Villa Madama

The uncompleted court surround, prior to recent restoration (photo. Alinari)

Guy Dewez

Villa Madama

A memoir relating to Raphael's project

Lund Humphries Publishers
London

First published in Great Britain in 1993 by
Lund Humphries Publishers Ltd
Park House
1, Russell Gardens
London NW11 9NN

British Library Cataloguing-in-Publication Data

A catalogue record for this book is available from the British Library

ISBN 0 85331 637 6

Designed by the Armelle Press
Typeset by Saxon Graphics Ltd
Printed & bound in Italy by Tipogrøfia Umbra on 135 gsm permanent paper   ↓ a

The author and publishers thank the following institutions for permission to reproduce illustrations in their possession: Albertina Museum, Vienna, Biblioteca Nazionale, Florence, Galleria degli Uffizi, Florence, and R.I.B.A. Drawings Collection, London.

Contents

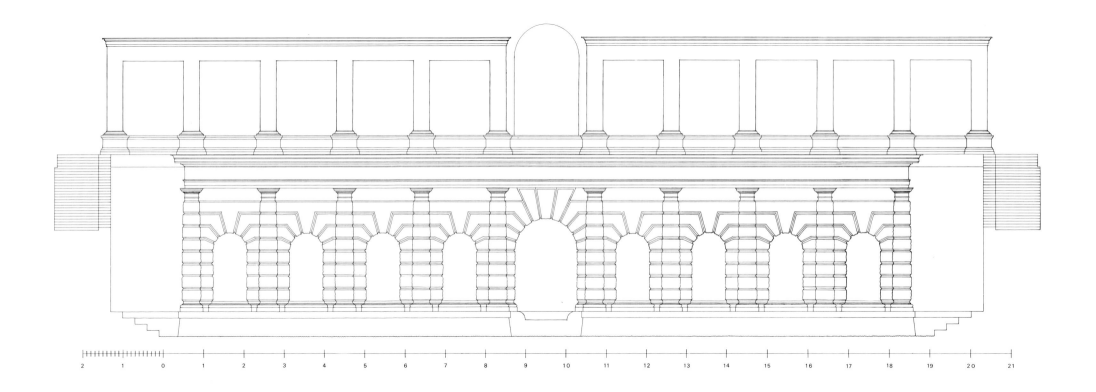

A reconstruction of the fishpond setting in Raphael's early project. (drawn by the author)

Prologue

Raphael must have had about two years to live when he was called upon to build the villa. At his death he had put one half of the project into execution but left no definite plans in respect of the other half. Yet a number of pointers exist as to his intentions and, purporting to show how he might have brought his project to completion, a model built to the present author's designs was displayed at the *Raffaello Architetto* exhibition held, in Rome, in 1984. The principal merit of the model, however, was to evidence the need for a continued reflection on the subject, an extended elicitation of the conceptual process involved, a discussion of the resulting implications and a partial revision of the conclusions originally arrived at. This account is a contribution to the task.

The work is divided into two main parts, the memoir and a series of illustrations with accompanying commentaries. A system of cross-references gives cohesion to the whole, the text paragraphs being numbered while the serial numbers of the figures appear at their appropriate place in the margins.

It is a revised version, substantially augmented, of that published in Rome, in 1990, under the title of *Villa Madama, Memoria sul Progetto di Raffaello*. Among other additions it contains a transcription, with a translation and running commentary, of the draft letter in which Raphael described his project, a chart relating to the unit of measurement employed by him, a large number of new illustrations and complementary evidence in respect of some of the conclusions finally come to. The illustration captions noted as G.D. refer to drawings made by the author.

The Memoir

1

Raphael was commissioned to build the villa by Cardinal Giulio de'Medici, first cousin of, and Secretary of State to, Pope Leo X, the head of the family[1]. Started late in 1518 construction was in progress when Raphael died, on April 6th, 1520. The work went on for a while after his death, under the direction of Giulio Romano, but was abandoned before half the scheme had been completed.

2

The project was a major undertaking of the early Cinquecento, second to none except the re-building of St Peter's. Proceeding from an idealization of the antique Roman villa, its purpose was evidently to provide an enchanting Medici residence at the gates of Rome where prominent visitors might be greeted, properly accommodated while making ready for their ceremonial entry and, during their stay in the city, lavishly entertained[2]. As a factor of Medici prestige it ranked with the contemporary Michelangelo commissions in Florence, the San Lorenzo façade project, the Medici Chapel and the Biblioteca Laurenziana. As a prospective Florentine landmark at the heart of the papal state it ranked with the project for San Giovanni dei Fiorentini.

3

The name of Madama comes from the pre-fixed title of Margaret of Austria, a natural daughter of Emperor Charles V, who became associated with the villa through her marriage to Alessandro de'Medici, Duke of Florence, in 1536[3]. Though she never owned the property personally her involvement continued after the death of her husband, assassinated in 1537, and her re-marriage to Ottavio Farnese, a nephew of Pope Paul III and future Duke of Parma, in 1539[4].

4

The incomplete state of the villa made it unfit for occupancy. After being used as an occasional place of entertainment it gradually lost much of its early appeal. In the course of time maintenance deteriorated. The villa had thus fallen into serious disrepair when, between 1913 and 1928, it underwent a renovation process aimed at making it habitable[5]. Having passed into state ownership, in 1940, and eventually been placed under the custody of the Ministry of Foreign Affairs it is currently used for state receptions and high-level meetings.

[1] Giulio de'Medici was to become Pope Clement VII, in 1523, following the death of Leo X and the brief pontificate of Adrian VI.

[2] Heads of State, Ambassadors, Princes of the Church, come to do hommage to the Pope, were accorded ceremonial entry into Rome. The celebrations lasted two days or more. Upon arrival the great personage would be met on the outskirts of the city – more often than not, close to Ponte Milvio – and escorted with his retinue to a suburban place of abode where he would sit in state, preside over the arrangements being made for his entry and spend the night or nights. The location of the villa would have made it highly suitable as such a stopping place. See D. Coffin: *The villa in the life of Renaissance Rome*, Princeton, 1979, and J. Shearman: 'A functional interpretation of Villa Madama', in *Römisches Jahrbuch für Kunstgeschichte*, XX, 1983, pp. 315 to 327.

[3] Alessandro de'Medici was reputedly the natural son of Giulio, himself the natural son of Giuliano, the brother of Lorenzo il Magnifico, assassinated in 1478.

[4] Owing to her imperial parentage and engaging personality Margaret enjoyed a great popularity in Rome. It was she who, some twenty years later, entrusted Vignola with the construction of that paradigm of princely palaces of Renaissance Italy, the Palazzo Farnese, in Piacenza.

[5] At the hands of two successive owners, a French businessman, M. Bergès, and an Italian nobleman, Count Dentice di Frasso. See R. Lefevre: *Villa Madama*, Rome, 1973.

[6] The plan is discussed and reproduced in A.P. Frutaz: *Le Piante di Roma*, Rome 1962, Plan CXCV, Vol. I, p. 262, Vol. III, pl. 502 to 506.

[7] Monte Mario has its summit at 139 metres.

[8] In order to regulate the flow of underground water a large barrel-vaulted drain was sunk into the hillside, about 10 metres above the villa, while damp-proofing was taken care of with the provision of dome-roofed segmental apses built against the buried side of the villa. These devices served their purpose for some considerable time but an entirely new system had to be put in recently: implemented by the Ministry of Works it was brought to completion in 1980.

5

The location of the villa, with its accesses and surroundings such as they existed prior to the urbanization of the area, may be seen in the detail of an 1839 plan reproduced in Fig. 1[6]. Flanking the north-eastern slopes of Monte Mario the villa stands about 1,500 metres from Ponte Milvio – the ancient Roman Pons Mulvius which, built in 109 BC, stood for 2,000 years as the outpost to Rome's principal gateway, Porta Flaminia – and 2,500 metres from both the Vatican and Piazza del Popolo. From the Vatican the road passed through an area of orchards and vineyards dotted with small rural buildings. At a distance of 2,000 metres a drive leading up to the villa forked off to the left while the road continued as far as Ponte Milvio. The intention was to run a straight drive from the centre of the villa down to the esplanade, North of Ponte Milvio, from where issued the ancient highways linking Rome with northern Italy and the rest of Europe. The drive was never executed.

6

The villa lies half-way up the hill, about 60 metres above sea-level[7]. From the site chosen the view covers a vast expanse of what was then open country. Ranging over the tree-tops, the meandering Tiber with its rush-covered banks, Ponte Milvio and its busy approaches, the eye wandered across the gently rising lowlands of Sabina to the mountainous background formed by the western slopes of the Apennines. To the North-West and North the view is limited by a tall outcrop of Monte Mario enclosing a shouldered coomb into which the gardens of the villa were meant to penetrate. To the South-East and South the view includes the Alban Hills and most of Rome. The longitudinal axis of the villa is 40 degrees off North. The main front thus faces North-East, the entrance front South-East, the opposite front North-West and the hill-side part South-West, the four corners facing either North, East, South or West.

7

Geologically Monte Mario belongs to a pleiocene formation of yellow sands and blue marls, rich in sea fossils. Highly absorbent and permeable the ground is soaked with moisture. Indeed the nature of the soil would have precluded the construction of a large structure had it not been for the presence of a shelf-like stratum of compact clay on which the foundations could be laid. The stratum is kept reasonably stable by the surrounding humidity but the underground part of the villa resting directly upon it can be compared to a dyke, with water filtering underneath. In other words the foundations are far from secure while the hillside position of the villa poses serious problems of damp-proofing and rain-water drainage[8].

8

The state the villa was left in may be seen in the measured drawings of a Grand Prix de Rome laureate, H.J.E. Bénard, dated 1871, reproduced in figs. 2 to 5, in the ancient photographs reproduced in figs. 6, 7, 8, 10 to 15,

[9] – Theobald Hofmann: *Raffael in seiner Bedeutung als Architekt*, I, Zittau, 1900.

[10] – The date of 1610 comes from a drawing published by F. Thone, in *Ein Deutschrömisches Skizzenbuch von 1609 – 1610*, Berlin, 1962. It is assumed that the tilting was due to a subsidence in the clay stratum.

[11] At both levels the width of the windows is 10 palmi or 2.234 metres. Obsolescent at the end of the Quattrocento, cross-window fenestration is hardly likely to have been revived by Raphael. Indeed, some of the joints in the windows overlooking the fishpond show that, contrary to normal practice, the mullions and transoms were inserted after the surrounds had been put in: see Fig 22. Yet, old-fashioned as they were, the fixtures had the merit of simplifying the task of window-framing. The decision to use them must have been taken when expediency came to prevail over other considerations in winding-up the work.

[12] Throughout the superstructure this is the only instance of vertical supports not resting upon an extension of the main order pedestal. It conforms with the jambs of the doorways shown in the right part of Fig. 49.

[13] A striking instance of extensive double-vaulting is that provided by Palazzo Te, in Mantua: see A. Belluzzi, W. Capezzali, *Il Palazzo dei Lucidi Inganni – Il Palazzo Te a Mantova*, Florence – Mantua, 1976.

[14] – In Raphael's initial project the window was in line with the longitudinal axis of the North-East loggia. Its re-positioning resulted from the squaring of the loggia terminations and the offsetting of the doorway leading into the North-West apartment.

[15] Decided upon following Raphael's death.

and in the measured drawings made by the architectural historian, Theobald Hofmann, at the end of the last century, some of which are reproduced in figs. 13, 15, 18, 23, 25 and 39[9].

9

The executed part of the villa consists of a ground-level basement, a superstructure which includes part of the circular court and loggia planned to stand at the centre of the complex, and a split-level continuation of the basement comprising a fishpond surmounted by a terrace-garden. The North-East front is adversely affected by a twin-arched buttress underlying the radiating arcade of the superstructure. Set up to counteract tilting, at some time or other before 1610 but probably quite soon after construction, it is a serious blemish[10]. So is the cross-window fenestration of the superstructure which was evidently put in after the death of Raphael, to save the trouble of duplicating the large timber frames of the basement windows[11]. Regarding the Bénard drawings, these are of special interest in showing first, in the executed part of the loggia, how the back-wall pilasters were to rest directly on the pavement[12] and second, in the cross-sections of the smaller superstructure rooms, how the compound rib-vaults supporting the attic-storey might have been underlaid with decorative vaults of reinforced stucco in the absence of the intermediary timber floors[13].

10

The North-West façade of the superstructure is the only one to have been completed. Strikingly asymmetrical owing to the hillside position of the villa, the dualistic composition features a windowed part overlooking the fishpond and a porticoed part corresponding to the terrace-garden with which it communicates. A highly disturbing particular is the median pilaster obstructing the spread of the windowed part. Absent from Raphael's initial project it was most probably introduced by Giulio Romano in relation to the re-positioning of the left-hand window[14]. The mezzanine windows proceed from yet another change made in the course of construction, the vertical subdivision of the smaller superstructure rooms[15]. Figs. 16 to 25 show various aspects and details of the villa as it stands today. The external effects of the renovation are particularly unfortunate, to wit the ill-designed columnated adjunction to the superstructure, the court-side trimmings above it and the openings cut into the segments of frieze underlying the main entablature. Adding fresh blemishes to the early ones they concur in turning the villa into an architectural jumble. Yet the noble proportions prevail, as does the imprint of a master's hand in the general design.

11

The North-East and North-West façades of the superstructure incorporate two kinds of bays, panelled and unpanelled, the latter being those of the North-West portico. The panels are bounded by an extrusion of the façade wall, part of which is inscribed within the radiating arcade of the North-East façade, while the rest is topped by the string-course delimiting the frieze segments under the entablature. Like the frieze segments,

[16] The difference in uprights is 1/3 palmo. This compares with a protrusion of the main order pilasters which is 1 palmo in relation to the basic wall surface, 2/3 palmo in relation to the extruded surface.

[17] Kept in the Uffizi: U 560/242 A.

[18] See P. Pagliara: 'Raffaello e la Rinascita delle Techniche Antiche', in *De Architectura – Les Chantiers de la Renaissance*, edited by A. Chastel and J. Guillaume, Paris, 1991, pp. 1-69.

[19] Discovered by P. Foster who was the first to publish and discuss the document: see 'Raphael on Villa Madama', in *Römisches Jahrbuch für Kunstgeschichte*, XI, 1967-1968, pp. 308-12.

[20] For an exhaustive account of the material relating to the planning and construction of the villa, see C.L. Frommel: 'Villa Madama', in *Raffaello Architetto*, edited by C.L. Frommel, S. Rai and M. Tafuri, Milan, 1984, pp . 311-356.

the field of the panels is on the same upright as that of the unpanelled bays. Consequently there are two wall surfaces, the basic surface of the unpanelled bays, the frieze segments and the field of the panels, the other being the extruded surface surrounding all the panelled bays[16]. Conveying a high degree of plasticity to the elevations the treatment is typical of Raphael's architectural work. Other instances are to be seen in Palazzo Pandolfini, Florence, and in a drawing of Raphael's studio for an architectural stage setting[17].

12

Before engaging into the discussion of the actual project a few words on the mode of construction employed are called for. All walls are in mortared tufa rubblework. Some are unfaced, others are faced with coursed rubblework or random rubble laid between brick courses. The superstructure walls have a carefully laid facing of alternating brick courses and coursed blocks of tufa, possibly inspired by late antique models[18]. For façades meant to be coated this type of facing has the double advantage of offering uneven surfaces for good purchase and clean-cut edges for the outlining of the wall protrusions. The vaults are constructed in a mortared aggregate of tufa. Travertine is used for bases, capitals and some of the mouldings. Brick is used as a stucco support for the other mouldings, with intercalated travertine guiding marks.

13

The general concept and over-all design of the villa are essentially known through two plans and a description of the project by Raphael himself, in the form of a draft letter[19]. Kept in the Uffizi the plans are designated by their inventory number preceded by the letter U, for Uffizi, and followed by the letter A, for Architettura, thus U 273 A and U 314 A respectively. They are reproduced in figs. 27 and 33. The first is by one of Raphael's assistants, Gianfrancesco da Sangallo, the second by Antonio da Sangallo il Giovane who, during the best part of Raphael's architectural career seems to have acted as his technical advisor. Chronologically , the U 273 A plan comes first, the description comes second and the U 314 A plan comes third[20]. Owing to the small scale of the plans – approximately 1 in 150 for the first and 1 in 350 for the second – they are both sketchy. Moreover, they contain a number of awkward details and corrections which suggest a certain degree of improvisation. Other original drawings and related documents are reproduced in figs. 26 to 38.

14

The U 273 A and U 314 A plans may be considered as variations on the same theme. Considered in the light of the actual building they both show an elongated rectangular complex, bulging out to contain a theatre on one of its long sides and subdivided into three main parts: in the centre, the superstructure enclosing a court connected with the theatre, on the South-East side an entrance court and a walled-in garden, on the North-West side the terrace-garden and the fishpond. They differ in several respects. The U 273 A plan, which belongs in the initial stage of the conceptual process, is based on a rectangular court the transversal sides of which are of different widths – the South-East side being considerably larger than its counterpart – while the entrance court is bordered with extensions of the superstructure. The U 314 A plan, which belongs in a

revisionary stage of the process, is centered on a circular court the transversal sides of which are of the same width while the entrance court is devoid of extensions. Affording substantially less accommodation, the second plan corresponds to the executed part of the villa. The project described by Raphael includes the circular court but is otherwise very close to the U 273 A plan: see Appendix A.

15

[21] Plans U 273 and U 314 A are reconstructed in accordance with the criteria set out in paragraphs 20, 22, 24, and in the commentaries to figs 44 and 53.

Raphael must have dictated his letter at a time when, having decided to substitute the circular to the rectangular court, he was still engaged in revising the South-East part of the project. Unwilling no doubt to disclose this, he described the part exactly as he had initially planned it thereby marking his intention to retain its main dispositions. Yet we shall see that far-reaching adjustments were called for which, indeed, were only partly contingent upon the introduction of the circular court. To this end we shall start by considering the South-East part of the U 273 A plan using, rather than the original, the reconstructed plan in which the principal rooms are marked from A to L[21].

27
53

16

Unlike the U 314 A plan, centred on the circular court, the U 273 plan is purely orthogonal. At its South-East end, the entrance court lies at the same level as the superstructure. Bordered on its North-East side by the walled-in garden and the corresponding return of the South-East side to the rectangular court, it is concluded at its North-West end by a monumental portico leading into the latter. Entering the court, on the left are grouped the staff dining-hall G, with its kitchen E, its larder F and a large storeroom D, all of which are set around a common entrance. On the right, about the domed hall, are grouped three square rooms H, I, J, followed by a pair of rectangular ones K, L, a large staircase rising from the bottom to the top of the edifice and a portico overlooking the walled-in garden. Together with the hall and the rooms surmounting them at the top level, these rooms were evidently to constitute the guest apartments. Their distribution is as brilliant as that of the service rooms D to G. It testifies to an acute sense of convenience and a planning skill which single out Raphael among his fellow architects.

53

17

The original of the U 273 A plan, however, displays a striking anomaly. Since the internal court does not include the set of ramps shown in the reconstructed plan there would have been no means of riding on horseback between the podium and superstructure levels. This is all the more surprising since high-ranking guests would, in most cases, have been expected to enter the villa via the monumental portal underlying the North-East loggia, at the end of the drive coming up from Ponte Milvio, and that etiquette required that such visitors and their retinue did not dismount before reaching the inner court. Moreover, the stables of the villa, were planned to stand at the level of the podium, in line with the North-East front of the complex, and would therefore not have been accessible from the entrance court placed at the superstructure level.

27
53

22 – With 5 risers of 3/4 palmo – a current size at the time – the height of the stairway would have reached 41 1/4 palmi, leaving 3/4 palmo for that of a sill at basement level. Taking into account the spread of the revolving steps, the average length of the stairways would have come to (23 × 2 = 46 × 2 = 92 palmi) + (8 × 2 1/2) = 20 palmi) = 112 palmi. As a matter of comparison with the gradients indicated that of Bramante's project for the Vatican 'Cordonata' is 28.60%.

18

It would indeed have been possible to convert into ramps the stairways backing the North-East loggia. Given the difference in levels of 42 palmi, the length of each stairway enclosure would have allowed the insertion of 54 treads, in two flights of 23 along the central spine, each tread being 2 palmi deep, plus 8 radial treads half-way up. But taken separately each enclosure would have been too short to accommodate a practicable set of ramps since the gradient would have reached about 37 % including the radial treads, 45% not including them[22]. A proper conversion would have required the merging of the two enclosures and the construction of a continuous ramp, twice returned, which would have passed under a bridge connecting the North-East loggia with the rectangular court. But such a solution would have been detrimental in two respects: by considerably increasing the walking distance between the two levels and by bringing into the villa the hustle and bustle of horse and mule traffic. Hence the ramps shown in the reconstructed plan which are based on a drawing by Giovan Francesco Penni, in the Albertina. But the presence of such a set of ramps in the court would have called for the provision, at podium level, of an extensive tunnel set along the transversal axis of the villa. It is quite likely, therefore, that it was the problem of internal transit which led Raphael to lower the level of the entrance court, thereby making it accessible from the South-East as well as from the North-East. A further advantage of the move was that it allowed the gradient of the drive coming up from the South-East to be substantially reduced.

19

The solution adopted may be seen in the reconstruction of the U 314 A plan. There are two parts to the entrance court, the lower part which is reached by means of a large fan-shaped ramp, and the grand stairway flanked by extrusions each of which contains a set of ramps giving access to the platform at the foot of the North-West façade. The internal wall of the walled-in garden being maintained, the North-West façade is subdivided into two sections, one backing the upper part of the entrance court, the other backing the walled-in garden. The former features a central portal in the form of a triumphal arch, the latter a portico recalling that of the U 273 A plan except that the arcades are replaced by columns. Devoid of pilasters, the design of the façade is therefore based on the juxtaposition of two separate elements, an exceptional arrangement of which the author knows no other example. The only problem posed is that of the wall surmounting the portico of the walled-in garden, which would have called for some kind of treatment. In any case, a high wall at the outer side of the walled-in garden was required to conceal the difference in the ordonnance of the South-East and North-East façades. It was also required, as Raphael insists upon in his description, to protect the garden from the winter winds: Appendix 1 paragraphs 7 and 13.

20

Let us now consider that part of the original U 314 A plan which relates to the superstructure. The plan is

33 most likely to have been drawn up by Sangallo, at Raphael's request, to help in solving the problems arising from the introduction of the circular court and the lowering of the entrance court. In the North-West half of the plan, which was put into execution, the inscribed dimensions are practically the same as those of the actual work. The reconstructed plan of the North-West portico and adjoining rooms aims at reproducing

41 Raphael's basic scheme: it is founded upon the executed work, on Raphael's description, on the U 314 A plan and on the observance of a strict consistency in the thicknesses given to the walls. Starting from there it

42 is likewise possible to reconstruct the basic plan of the North-East loggia, that of the North-West half of the

43 complex minus the theatre and the North tower and, finally, to turn out the reconstruction of the U 314 A plan. Regarding the latter it is to be observed that the two median axes of the passage leading from the North-

44 East loggia into the circular court happen to be exactly of the same length thereby corroborating the accuracy of the dimensions adopted.

21

Reverting to the U 314 A plan, there are two series of questions to be examined: the first relates to the changes introduced in the course of construction, the second to the consequences of the substitution of the circular to the rectangular court and of the lowering of the entrance court.

22

Some of the changes made in the course of construction are perceptible in the U 314 A plan. This is the

33 case with the external walls of the two rooms at the back of the portico. Unlike that of their counterparts in the South-East part of the plan, the inner side of these walls is not tangent to the wall of the circular court. It was shifted inward thereby allowing secondary staircases to be inserted into the thickness of the walls whereas, the width of the rooms remaining unchanged, the corresponding side of the opposite walls was shifted as far as possible in the direction of the North-West portico. The arrangement caused the centre of curvature of the apsidal recesses to be placed in line with their outer side, in contradiction with Raphael's usual practice which, in the present case, would have been to place the centre in line with the inner side of the bordering pilaster. But it also resulted in providing sufficient space for a passage to be cut slantwise into the wall thickness at the East corner of the portico. All these dispositions evidently answered a wish of the patron to see additional accommodation provided above the rooms marked 1,2 and 4 in the reconstructed plan,

41 plus another above room 5. As we have seen in paragraph 10 *supra*, the adjunction implied the substitution of timber ceilings for the vaults of rooms 1, 2, 4 and 5. Moreover it seriously impaired the integrity of

44 the scheme and, consequently, has not been taken into account in the reconstructed plans.

23

Similar changes came from the squaring of the North-East loggia terminations, originally meant to be apsidal

recesses, and the provision of end walls bearing a raised niche set between twin doorways. One of these doorways being a sham, the doorway between rooms 3 and 2 was put in line with the true one and, to increase the enfilade effect, the North-West window of room 2 was shifted into a position as close as possible to the North-East façade wall. The result was to throw the windowed part of the North-West façade out of balance and cause the introduction of the median pilaster referred to in paragraph 10 *supra*. Though Raphael was most probably not the initiator of this last move – but may have agreed to it – the squaring of the loggia terminations was certainly of his own making. The decision was too important to have been taken by anyone 27 else added to which the end wall design was obviously a transfer from that of the end wall of the North-West portico, in the U 273 A plan.

24

Let us now examine how the introduction of the circular court and the lowering of the entrance court affected the general scheme. The adoption of the circular court, evidently meant to appear as the heart of the complex, necessarily called for a centralization of the plan, if not transversally owing to the hillside position of the villa, at least longitudinally. This was achieved through the correlative reduction in the longitudinal spread of the court which brought about an equalization in the widths of its South-East and North-West sides thereby making the outer façades of both equidistant from the centre. On the other hand, the transversal spread of the court being augmented entailed a radical change in the stairways backing the North-East loggia. 44 Described by Raphael as being both triangular, so are they shown in the reconstruction of the U 314 A plan. With 2 palmi treads and 3/4 palmo risers, each numbers 53 treads plus two intermediary landings, the corresponding number of risers coming to 56 which means that the difference in levels of 42 palmi would have been entirely filled without the provision of a sill at the basement entrance. In this connection it should also be noted that, in the original of the U 314 A plan, the triangular stairway stops at the superstructure level. Consequently, the sole access to the upper level would have been by means of the staircase adjoining the staff dining-hall, the upward continuation of the secondary court-side staircases being impossible to maintain in the finished building owing to the inadequate height of the court wall. Such is the reason why, prior to construction being abandoned, the projected flights of the stairway were returned in order to allow 7 their further deployment to reach the upper level at the very place where the corridor leading from the South-East to the North-West side of the court would have ended.

25

In the U 314 A plan, Sangallo did away with the wings bordering the entrance court in the U 273 A project. Hence he considerably reduced the importance of the guest apartments and brought to nought the beautiful 33 arrangement of the staff quarters. He even arrived at the following absurdity. Having cut down the accommodation to a bare minimum consisting of the hall and storeroom, plus a small nondescript room, thereby assigning all cooking activities to the hall proper, he placed the one and only storeroom doorway

inside the passage leading from the circular court to the theatre. It follows that all supplies being brought into
44 or taken out of the storeroom would have passed through the entrance portico, the vestibule and the circular
court, in that order or the reverse. In the reconstructed plan, the hall, the store room and the nondescript
room have been made to communicate but the closeness of the openings hardly improves matters.

26

Another serious defect in Sangallo's plan is the extravagant lengthening of the walled-in garden coupled with
the scrapping of its outer wall meant to afford protection against the winter winds, this last move making the
garden porticoes look like fortuitous appendages and exposing the unfortunate contrast between the plain
wall surmounting the portico and the ordonnance of the North-East façade. Indeed, the great weakness in
Sangallo's plan comes from the fact that its author, bent on extolling the constraints of centralization,
apparently failed to realize that it was perfectly admissible to retain the side wings of the court provided they
were differenciated from the superstructure. Raphael would certainly not have allowed himself to be misled
in such a matter and it is highly probable that his project, once completed, would have been akin to that
which he described. It remains to be imagined what such a project might have looked like.

27

The superstructure elevations, reproduced in Fig. 48, proceed from an adaptation of the execution scheme
to the plan dimensions defined in the commentaries to figs. 40 A and B, 41 and 42.
The interruptions in the string-course underlying the main entablature come from the façade treatment
described in paragraph 11 *supra*, the string-course forming a conclusion to the wall surfaces which surround
the panels. In the arcaded bays of the North-West portico and the screen bays of the loggia, the jambs of the
arches are on the same upright as the field of the panels thereby excluding an extension of the panelling into
the spandrel areas. Likewise, the lower part of the niche bay next to the loggia is on the same upright as the
panel surrounds, the upper part on that of the field in the panelling. The animation of the façades, the size
55B and variety of the areas made available for decorative purposes, all concur to make the design vastly superior
to that of the initial project in which the generalization of the double wall surfaces looks rather academic.

28

With their depressed cornice and heavy surround – the thickness of the latter amounting to one fifth of the
22 aperture width – the inset windows of the superstructure are particularly stocky. They obviously derive from
29 the original mezzanine windows in the interior of the Pantheon of which Raphael made a drawing in his
30 formative years as an architect. Yet there is a considerable difference between the two: in the case of the
Pantheon the enframing pilasters are less than one and a quarter times as high as the window whereas, in that
of the villa, they are over two and a half times. In the first case the edges of the window overlap the pilasters,
in the second it is the contrary, the result being that in the villa the horizontal mouldings of the pilaster and

[23] Excellently analyzed by P.N. Pagliara: 'Palazzo Branconio', in *Raffaello Architetto, op. cit.* pp. 197-210. *Id.*: 'Due Palazzi Romani di Raffaello', in *Raffaello a Roma, II Convegno del 1983*, Rome, 196, pp. 331-342.

[24] The reason for not re-locating the window of room 1 in the same way as that of room 2 is unclear. Internally the effect produced would have been akin to that in room 2 added to which the offsetting of such a large window would have been of little consequence in the lighting of the room.

[25] Evidenced by the changes operated in the course of construction, most of them detrimental. They suggest that Giulio de'Medici had very much come to look upon the villa as a private place of his own, far removed from its original purpose.

36
37
pillar bases collide with the vertical mouldings of the window surrounds. The maladjustment is all the more surprising if one considers the pains taken to obviate a similar one in the court façades of Raphael's almost contemporary Palazzo Branconio da L'Aquila[23].

29

36
48
A comparison of the executed work with a studio drawing by Giulio Romano raises the question as to why, in such an important work as the villa, Raphael should have ignored design contingencies which he had respected elsewhere. This is even more incomprehensible if one considers the additional problem posed in the North-East façade where the window cornices had to be truncated to avoid an interference with the niche at the centre of the radiating arcade. At the time of Raphael's death the façades of the apartment were going up and the window of room 2 had been re-located while that of room 1 had not, thereby motivating the introduction of the median pilaster referred to in paragraph 10 *supra*[24]. Raphael may have been considering a substitute for the problematical window, yet again he may not: possibly feeling the strain of his multiple activities, possibly becoming weary of his patron's incessant meddling[25], or possibly sensing that the villa enterprise was too ambitious to be brought to completion, he may just as well have given Giulio Romano a free hand in the matter. Whatever the circumstances, it is hard to believe that, of his own volition, Raphael should have persisted in the implementation of such a window.

30

38
A substitute he might have adopted is that which incorporates a surroundless aperture and a detached cornice such as may be seen in the decorative work he carried out in the second storey loggia of the Vatican, in the years 1518-1519. The motif was used by Michelangelo in his San Lorenzo façade project of 1516-1517, as well as by Giulio Romano himself, following Raphael's death, in Villa Lante al Gianicolo. Clearly belonging in the architectural vocabulary of the period, it has the advantage of meeting all the requirements of the façade design: consequently, it has been incorporated into the illustrative material grouped under Section Six *infra*.

27
Regarding the balusters of the North-East loggia, the way they are aligned in a single row above the basement portal reproduces the U 273 A arrangement. Although Raphael mostly used double-bulbed balusters, these have been made single-bulbed for reasons of scale and solidity.

31

57
The central part of the tentative completion plan differs from the corresponding part of the U 314 A plan in the following respects. The staff quarters having been reinstated in accordance with Raphael's description and the U 273 A plan, the storeroom, in 8, is entered through a vestibule which also gives access, in 9, to the kitchen followed by the larder and, in 10, to the dining hall at the side of which climbs the stairway leading up to the attic. The entrance portico and lobby, both of the same length and barrel-vaulted, are separated by a 5 palmi thick arcade. The portico is aisled and columnated, the lobby is pilastered, but the number of

columns and pilasters has been brought up from four to six, this for the following reasons. The first is that six is the figure indicated by Raphael for the number of columns inside the portico, the second that a subdivision into even numbers of the bays formed by the pilasters lining the aisles of the portico and by those lining the lobby is in keeping with the paired lengths of the double passageway and, the third, that the resulting intercolumniations equal the classical 2 1/4 column diameters whereas the Sangallo intercolumniation is unduly wide. In room 1, the window has been placed in a position corresponding to that of the window in room 2, thereby allowing the median pilaster to be removed and the ordonnance of the U 273 A design to be restored. Finally, in keeping with Raphael's concern with convenience, a means of communication between rooms 1 and 4 has been provided by way of room 3.

32

In the North-West part of the executed work, the extruded stairways leading down from the fishpond are
2 interrupted in mid-air and turned inwards by means of tunneled returns, thereby saving the space required
3 for outward returns and making the fishpond platforms large enough for one of them to be used as an open-
5 air dining area. The lopsided arrangement evidently answered yet another afterthought of the patron[26]. It is a
clever contrivance, but a contrivance all the same, which incorporates the following anomalies: a descending
11 movement not balanced by an ascending one, an incongruously narrow stairway extrusion, a pronounced
offsetting of the passage leading into the tunneled part of the stairway and, finally, an extrusion façade which
21 is out of scale with the rest of the composition. Affecting the integrity of the design the arrangement has not
been taken into account in the tentative completion scheme, any more than the shifting of the longitudinal
walls in rooms 4 and 5. Consequently, the stairways are shown outwardly returned.

33

The South-East part of the tentative completion scheme is that which departs most from the U 314 A plan.
57 Conforming to Raphael's description and the U 273 A plan, the wings bordering the entrance court have
60 *A* been retained, the differentiation requirement being met by making their walls somewhat lower than those
of the superstructure. The North-West extension of the storeroom engendered by the circular court gives room, in the South-West wing, to increase the size of the vestibule thereby making it fit to accommodate the unloading of pack-beasts. On the opposite side, the wing has been made to contain three rooms comparable in size with rooms 1 to 3, plus three similar rooms above and a stairway connecting both storeys with the baths in the basement. At superstructure level, the major room opens into a columnated and terrace-surmounted portico fronting the walled-in garden, the latter being fitted with a wall-clinging stepped gangway leading up to the terrace overlying the portico. There is no documentary justification for the insertion of this last feature which has the disadvantage of calling for a tunneled access to the East tower passing through the bent part of the gangway. But it palliates the one and only inadequacy in Raphael's plan which comes from he fact that the walled-in garden, meant to be half as wide as the entrance court, does not allow sufficient space for the provision of a proper wall to form part of the North-East façade[27]. Raphael

[26] In his description of the fishpond Raphael mentions an open air dining area, strangely located at the foot of the North-West stairway, but there is no trace of it in the U 273 A plan which in all other respects closely matches the text. Yet it was certainly not a matter of open-air dining which led Raphael to change his plan. In this case the patron has good cause to reject the proposed scheme, which was that of an antique natatio, or swimming pool, and as such would have been in contradiction with the spiritual character of ornamental garden design in ancient Rome. At the time of drafting his description Raphael had obviously not yet revised this part of his project. When he did, he provided good-sized platforms at both ends of the fishpond though, most probably, with outwardly returned stairways. The dimensions of the platforms would then have been 44 by 45 palmi – or 9.83 by 10.05 metres – less a corner indentation of 6 by 10 palmi – or 1.34 by 2.23 metres – due to a four-stepped ultimate return of the stairway. In the case of the executed work the planned dimensions were brought up to 45 by 54 palmi – or 10.05 by 12.06 metres – and it is undoubtedly with this end in view that the stairways were returned inwardly.

27 Hence, in the U 273 A as well as in the U 314 A plans, the wall being shown as a parapet.

could not have ignored the problem and certainly intended to take care of it at the appropriate moment. The author's solution has the merit of enlivening the South-East and North-East walls of the garden.

34

Before bringing this review to a close, a few more words are required concerning the entrance court design and the length of the wings. The design is evidently Sangallo's who may or may not have been following Raphael's directives. It is not a good design. In the first place it was unworkable as drawn, a serious change in the proportions of the bipartite scheme being necessary. But its main fault lies in the general concept which privileges a pedestrian access to the superstructure, via the grand stairway, at the expense of the accesses destined for mounted persons who, followed by their retinue, would have had to trudge their way up twice returned enclosed ramps and, upon reaching a comparatively narrow platform, dangerously edging the precipitous stairway, make a double 90-degree turn to enter the portico. On the other hand, the court's subdivision inappropriately limits the length of the wings thereby making the North-East one visually too short with regard to the rest of the façade. As shown in the completion scheme, the deficency could be remedied by extending the wing to incorporate the walled-garden portico, but it is clear that taking such a step should have been preceded by a complete re-designing of the court, probably centered upon a large ramp set along the longitudinal axis of the villa, with platforms at its sides, enclosing the stairways.

35

The illustrations with their commentaries follow the appendices. They are grouped under six sections. Section One deals with the villa as it stood prior to its renovation, early in the present century, while Section Two deals with the villa as it stands to-day. Section Three relates to the original plans and other documents used in the discussion. Section Four concerns the design put into execution by Raphael. It contains a tentative reconstruction and a further discussion of the scheme, including such changes introduced in the course of construction as may have been worked out by Raphael's assistants and accepted by him, to wit the addition of the median pilaster and the inward returning of the fishpond stairways. It does not include the most detrimental change, evidently made to suit the personal conveniences of Giulio de'Medici: the incorporation of mezzanine rooms over rooms 1, 2, 4 and 5. Section Five concerns the early project of Raphael, the basement part of which was executed. It also contains a reconstruction and further discussion, this time relating to a scheme which was entirely of Raphael's own making and the first to evidence his outstanding ability as a planner. Section Six contains the tentative completion scheme of the project discussed in Section Four. It incorporates a substitute for the design of the questionable superstructure window. It discards the median pilaster and restores the fishpond stairways to normality. Regarding the South-East part of the project it strives to make the best of Sangallo's design but there is no doubt that, had Raphael lived and had the project been brought to completion, the entrance court would have looked very different.

Appendix 1
Raphael's description of his project

The document is a draft letter the addressee of which may have been Baldassare Castiglione. It is kept in the Archivio di Stato, Florence, where it is filed as follows : Archivio Mediceo avanti il Principato, Filza 94, n° 162, cc 294–299.

The transcription of the Italian text, divided into paragraphs, with a spelling which has been made more consistent than in the original, is based on that published by Renato Lefevre, in *Studi Romani*, 1969, pp. 433–437. Numbered 01 to 26, the paragraphs are each followed by an English translation and a commentary in the form of notes. Evidently taken under dictation the original is not without some awkward phrasing and repetitions. In the translation an attempt has been made to minimize the effects of both and, rather than try and conform with the ancient mode of expression, to make the description as readily intelligible as possible. The most extreme case of a change in the articulation of the original text will be found in the translation of the first paragraph hereunder.

1 – *La villa è posta a mezo la costa di Monte Mario che guarda per linea recta a grecho. Et perch'el monte gira, dalla parte che guarda Roma scopre il mezo di et da la opposita scopre maestro et alle spalle del monte restano lybicco et ponente in modo che questa villa ha, de otto venti, sei che la tochano e son questi cioè hostro, syroccho, levante et greco, et tramontana et maestro : a che V.S. può considerare come gira il sito. Ma per porre la villa a venti piu sani ho volta la sua lungheza per diretta linea a syroccho e a maestro, con questa advertentia che a syroccho non venghano finestre nè habitatione alcune, se non quelle che ànno di bisogno del caldo.*

1 – The villa lies half-way up the north-eastern slope of Monte Mario. Abutted by high ground stretching South-West and West, the hill curves round from its Rome-looking side, which faces South, to that facing North-West. Consequently, out of the eight winds six affect the villa which are the following : Austro (South), Sirocco (SE), Levante (East), Greco (NE), Tramontana (North) and Maestrale (NW)[1]. This will enable Your Lordship to understand the lie of the land. To have the villa face the most salutary winds I have disposed it lengthwise on a South-West/North-East axis minding that there should be no windows nor any accommodation facing South-East except where warmth is required[2].

1[1] – The other two are Libeccio (SW) and Ponente (West).

1[2] – The question of orientation is treated by Vitruvius, in Book I, Chapter XI, and in Book VI, Chapter VI. Considering the site, Raphael could hardly have given the villa a different orientation. Regarding south-eastern exposure, Raphael would have been more correct in saying that he limited it as much as possible and, when unavoidable, tried to put it to good use.

2[1] – In the original the word used is Palace meaning the Vatican. The Prati – the Meadows – was the name given to the alluvial ground forming the right bank of the Tiber between the Vatican and Monte Mario : though the area is now thickly built over the designation still applies.

2[2] – Ponte Molle was one of the names given to Ponte Milvio, originally Pons Mulvius, in the course of its long existence. The road only existed by the riverside, close to the bridge, where it formed part of the road connecting the Vatican with the junction of the North and East-bound ancient Roman highways referred to in the Introduction.

2[3] – The acute angle formed between the road and the bridge makes the assertion rather unconvincing.

3[1] – This signifies that the villa was originally meant to be entered at its main, not at its lower level. It is of vital importance for the understanding of the U 273 A plan.

3[2] – Evidently under the influence of the Younger Pliny's description of his own villa, Raphael indulges here in a little wishful thinking. In fact, the direct climb from the Prati to the main level of the villa would have been quite stiff. To obtain an access such as Raphael describes would have called for the construction of a road skirting the hillside over some considerable distance. This clearly caused the transfer of the entrance from the main to the lower level but, even so, the road gradient would have been fairly high.

4[1] – Large towers is the translation of *Torrioni*. Henceforth, in the Italian text, each one of these structures is referred to as *Turrione* which means bastion and applies to their lower part.

4[2] – The dimensions are those of the U 273 A plan.

4[3] – In the U 273 A plan, there are four columns instead of six. The Italian text specifies that the columns are round, probably to avoid a confusion with square pillars.

2 – *Et ha questa villa due entrate principale, l'una per una via che vi si viene da Palazo et per lli Prati et l'atra per recta linea va a Ponte Molle, de novo facta, l'una e l'atra larghe 5 canne, e direste veramente Ponte Molle essere fatto per questa villa perché la strada arriva proprio al ponte. Et in capo a questa strada è una gran porta che sta collocata in mezo allo edifitio.*

2 – The villa has two principal entrances. One faces the road coming from the Vatican, across the Prati[1], the other a new road going straight to Ponte Milvio[2]. Both are 5 canne wide. Since the second actually ends at Ponte Milvio it makes it look as though the bridge had been built for the villa[3]. At the head of this road a large portal stands in the middle of the edifice.

3 – *Ma per non dare confusione a V.S. in narrarvi le sue parte, commincerò alla intrata della via che vien da Palazo e lli Prati, la quale è principale entrata e non nella costa del monte, più alta che quella de Ponte Molle quatro canne : et salisce tanto dolcemente che non pare de salire, ma essendo giunto alla villa non se accorgie de essere in alto e de dominare tutto il paese.*

3 – To avoid confusing Your Lordship I shall start my description by the entrance facing the Vatican and Prati road. It is the main entrance of the villa. Standing clear of the hillside, it lies 4 canne above the level of the Ponte Milvio entrance[1]. Yet the rise in the road is so gentle that the villa is reached before it is realized that one has ascended considerably and come to dominate the entire countryside[2].

4 – *Et sono nella prima apparentia di là et de qua de questa entrata doi torrioni tondi che, oltra la belleza et superbia que dànno alla intrata, servano anchora a un pocho de difesa a cui vi si riduce; tra li quali una bellissima porta dorica fa intrata in un cortile lungo 22 canne e largho 11. In testa del quale cortile vi è il vestibulo a modo et usanza antiqua con sei colonne tonde hyoniche con le lore ante, come recerca la ragione sua.*

4 – The main characteristic of the entrance is that it is set between two large circular towers which make it both handsome and forbidding while permitting some defence in case of need[1]. In the centre is a very fine Doric portal leading into a court, measuring 22 by 11 canne, at the head of which is a vestibule[2]. Conforming in lay-out and destination with the usage of Antiquity, this vestibule features six Ionic columns complete with their *antae* as Your Lordship would expect[3].

5 – *Da questo vestibulo s'entra nel atrio fatto alla greca, come quello che li thoscani chiamano andrione per mezo del quale l'homo se conduce in nun cortile tondo tondo, il quale horaculo lascio per non confondere, et torno a dire le parte et habitatione del primo cortile. Et perché questo tene del syroccho e mezo di, vi è la cucina e la dispensa e 'l tinello publico. Et poi vi è una cantina cavata nel monte, la quale serve a questi tali lochi publici, ma li suoi lumi sono volti a tramontana : loco freschissimo, come V.S. pò comprendere.*

5 – From the vestibule one passes into an Atrium in the Greek style[1], or *Androne* in the Italian sense, and thence into a circular court the orbicular character of which I shall not discuss here to save complicating matters[2]. Instead, I shall return to the first court and describe its parts. Since it looks to the South-East and South, it is here that one will find the household kitchen, the butcher's shop and the common dining hall[3]. A store-room, hollowed out of the hillside and lit from the North, completes this part of the household quarters[4]. As Your Lordship may imagine, it is a very cool place indeed.

6 – *Queste cose sono tutte tra 'l vestibulo e il monte, a man sinistra quando s'entra. Dalla dextra vi è un bello giardino di melangholi, di lungheza de 11 canne et 5½ largho, e tra questi melangholi è in mezo una bella fontana d'acqua che per diverse vie arriva quivi, sospinta et presa dalla sua viva vena.*

6 – The part just mentioned is located between the vestibule and the hillside, on the left as one enters. On the right is a beautiful garden planted with sour-orange-trees and measuring 11 by 5 ½ canne[1]. In the centre of the garden, among the trees, is a fine fountain fed with spring-water which arrives there under its own strong pressure by means of various conduits[2].

7 – *Sopra il turrione che è da man diritta della intrata, ne l'angulo, una bellissima dietha vi è conlochata, che così la chiamano li antiqui, la forma della quale è tonda et per diametro è 6 canne con uno andito per venirne, come al suo luoco ragionero, el quale copre detto giardino dal vento greco; da tre parti dello edifitio lo coprano da tramontana et maestro.*

7 – The bastion at the right of the entrance supports a very attractive structure such as the Ancients called *Diaeta*[1]. Built on a circular plan it has a diameter of 6 canne[2] and, as I shall explain, is reached by way of a corridor protecting the garden from the Greco (NE)[3]. It is further protected from the Tramontana (N) and Maestrale (NW) by the rest of the edifice.

5[1] – The reference to an Atrium in the Greek style comes from a misinterpretation of Vitruvius, Book VI, Chapter IX.

5[2] – The word Horaculo in the Italian text, meaning an oracle and, by extension, the innermost part of a sanctuary, is senseless. It most probably stands for the Latin Orbiculus which means a disk. What Raphael spares us here is obviously a discourse on the esoteric significance of the circular shape.

5[3] – All this conforms with the U 273 A plan.

5[4] – The sleeping quarters were to occupy the attic storey : see 25 *infra*.

6[1] – Melangolo is the *Citrus Bigaradia*, or sour-orange-tree, the fruit of which is currently known as the Seville Orange, used to make marmalade. Grown trees average a height of 3.00 to 3.50 m. Throughout the present work this particular garden is referred to as the walled-in garden.

6[2] – The spring must be that shown in the top left-hand corner of the main level Bénard plan reproduced in Fig. 2.

7[1] – The word Diaeta probably comes from the Younger Pliny. At his time of writing, it meant a detached or semi-detached structure occupying a privileged position in a villa complex and enclosing a room or a suite of rooms. In such a sense it applies perfectly here, but we shall see that Raphael also uses it to designate certain amenities in the main block.

7[2] – With a 6 p. thick wall, the internal diameter would have been 48 p. making the room one of the largest in the villa. In the U 273 A and U 314 A plans, the diameter is brought down to 30 p. internally and 40 p. externally. With its centre placed at the intersection of parallels to the outer walls of the superstructure, 6 palmi away, the larger structure has eight windows corresponding to the main points of the compass, with the western window overlooking the walled-in garden. The smaller structure only has seven windows since the emplacement of the western window is taken up by the entrance from the corridor. In the elevations, reproduced in Figs 55 and 56, the larger structure naturally looks far more impressive. Though there is no evidence for the crenellation shown, Raphael's description of the main entrance gives it some plausibility: see 4 *supra*.

7[3] – In the U 273 A and U 314 A plans, the sides of the corridor are so thin as to make them look like parapets. The indication given here clearly shows that walls were intended. The discrepancy results from a miscalculation of the space required: see paragraph 33 of the memoir.

8[1] – Clear glass panes were only just coming into use.

8[2] – To such an end the larger structure would have been much more suitable. The smaller, with its diameter of 30 p. or 6.705 m., is in the nature of a large study.

9[1] – Loggia is translated as portico since the word applies to a three-sided enclosure communicating with a garden and directly related to it, that of loggia normally applying to a similar enclosure set off the ground. According to the U 273 A plan, the portico forms the lower part of the NE wing at the entrance end of the edifice or superstructure.

9[2] – This naturally applies to a person entering the superstructure from the walled-in garden, not from the entrance court.

10[1] – In the executed work as well as in the U 314 A plan, the diameter of the court is 148 palmi instead of 150. This part of Raphael's description is of paramount importance for our understanding of the planning development. By assigning the circular court to the middle of the edifice he evidences the fact that, at the time of dictating his description, he was already working on the centralized scheme represented in the U 314 A plan.

10[2] – The flight width of 11 palmi is that of the spine-walled, single revolution stairways of the U 273 A plan. The spread of the circular court caused the flight width of the triangular stairways to be brought down to 8 palmi.

8 – La dietha è, come ho detto, tonda et ha intornno intorno finestre invetriate le quale hor l'una hor l'altra dal nascente sole al suo occaso serano toche et traspaiano in modo che 'l loco sarà alegrissimo et per il continuo sole et per lla veduta del paese et de Roma, perché, come V.S. sa, il vetro piano non occuperà alcuna parte. Sarà veramente questo loco piacevolissimo a starvi d'inverno a ragionare con gentilhomini, ch'è l'uso che sol dare la dietha. Et questa è quanto si fa ne l'un capo del giardino et nel suo angulo.

8 – As I have just said, the Diaeta is a circular structure. It is lit through a ring of glass windows, each of which is successively visited by the sun from the time it rises until it sets. Plane glass being no hindrance, as Your Lordship knows, it follows that the room is made exceedingly agreeable by the constant sunshine and the panorama of town and country[1]. In winter-time, it will serve its purpose as a delightful place in which to hold polite conversation[2]. This takes care of one end of the garden and the corresponding angle of the villa.

9 – Da l'atro capo verso l'habitatione, vi è una lhoggia a servitio pur dello inverno, che è volta a syroccho e a mezo dì; et alla habitatione vi si viene dentro e non dal primo cortile, anchor che vi sia a lato. Anzi da epso cortile non si può vedere la lhoggia né 'l giardino né la dietha, per un muro interposto che fa parete da'lato dextro del primo cortile. Et questo è quanto è nelli quatro lati del primo cortile.

9 – At the opposite end, on the dwelling side, is a portico[1] facing South-East and South, made for winter use. It is through it that one enters the dwelling, not through the first court though they lie side by side[2]. Indeed, from the court one cannot see either the portico, the garden or the Diaeta, since there is a wall in between. So much for the four sides of the first court.

10 – El secondo cortile, ch'è in nel mezo dello edifitio, è tondo e 'l suo diamitro è di 15 canne et ha da man dextra una gran porta dritta a greco, simile a quella della entrata in epso, la quale porta da ogni lato truova una schala trianghulare et la largheza è 11 palmi, la quale salita ha intrata in uno andrione lungo quanto che è due branche delle schale. Et questo dà intrata nel mezo d'una bellissima lhoggia, la quale guarda dritto a greco et è per longheza 14 canne, largha 3 et alta 5.

10 – The second court, in the middle of the edifice, is circular and has a diameter of 15 canne[1]. On the right stands a portal, open to the Greco (NE), similar to that by which one enters. On each side of the aperture is a triangular stairway. The flights are 11 palmi wide and issue from a lobby as long as twice the width of a flight[2]. This lobby leads into a splendid loggia, fronting the Greco (NE), which measures 14 by 3 canne and is 5 canne high[3].

10[3] – We are now back with the U 273 A design except that, in the plan, the width of the loggia is marked 32 palmi instead of 30. The height of 5 canne is an average. In the executed work, the figure applies to the interval between the main level and the level of the attic storey. Allowing a minimum of 2 palmi for the thickness of the vault at its apogee, the internal height of the loggia should not exceed 48 palmi. But the central dome of the NW portico breaks through the attic storey floor level, and such would certainly have been the case here. The length of 14 canne is that of the U 273 A loggia : in the U 314 A plan, it is brought up to 146 palmi.

11 – *Da omne capo de questa lhoggia vi è uno bellissimo nichio. La facciata è partita in tre archature. L'arco del mezo è tutto vano et esci fora sopra un poco de uno turrione quadro con li parapetti intorno, il quale fa porta di sotto. Da questo luoco si può vedere per retta linea la strada que va dalla villa al Ponte Molle, el bel paese, el Tivere et Roma.*

11 – At both ends of the loggia is a very fine apsidal recess[1]. The façade is made up of three arcades. Each of the side arcades encloses a pair of Doric columns[2] while the central arcade is completely open. Resting upon a square-angled bastion serving as the ground level portal and surmounted by a balustrade, the central arcade stands slightly forward from the façade alignment[3]. From here, one may see the road to Ponte Milvio straight ahead[4], the beautiful countryside, the Tiber and Rome[5].

12 – *A pié di questa lhoggia se extende lo hypodromo, come V.S. intenderà, il quale harà di lungheza quanto la villa se extende verso syroccho et maestro. Li dui altri archi della lhoggia hanno partito il lor vano con due colonne tonde doriche. Da l'un delli capi della lhoggia, a man diritta verso syroccho, per una parte ch'è in nel mezo al nichio s'entra in una bellissima et grande sala la quale ha cinque fenestre volte a greco et guardano sopra lo hypodromo et è la sala 8 canne e mezo lungha et largha 5 canne e mezo, et ha quatro archi che la reduchano in forma quadra et in mezo fa una volta tonda a uso de cupola et la sua alteza è 7 canne.*

12 – As Your Lordship will understand, at the foot of the loggia lies the hippodrome[1]. It extends the whole length of the villa, from its North-West to its South-East ends. At the South-East end of the loggia, a doorway in the centre of the apsidal recess opens into a vast and magnificent hall with five windows looking North-East across the hippodrome. The hall is 8½ *canne* long, 5½ *canne* wide. It is vaulted by means of four arcades forming a square and supporting a hemispheric dome 7 *canne* high[2].

13 – *Da questa sala si va in cinque camere, due che voltano a greco, una al monte et ha il lume dal primo cortile, l'altra a syroccho, et medesimamente responde sopra il primo cortile, l'atra a maestro, la qual responde sopra il cortile tondo. De queste camere, tre sono di buona grandeza, l'atre due più piccole un pocho. Le prime tre sono di 4 canne. In fin di queste camere vi è una schala secreta per andare nelle stanze de basso et quelle di sopra fatte per lla famiglia. Di qui si va ancora nella lhoggia ditta, volta a mezo dì, et al giardinetto de li melangholi et alla dietha per un andito, come di sopra vi dissi.*

13 – From the hall one comes to a succession of five rooms. Two are lit from the North-East, two from the entrance court – one looking to the hill, the other facing South-East – and one from the circular court[1]. Three of these rooms are comparatively large, the other two somewhat smaller, the first being 4 *canne* square. Beyond these rooms a private stairway leads down to the ground level and up to the household quarters at the top of the edifice[2]. From here one enters the SE portico, the sour-orange-tree garden and, by way of the corridor I mentioned earlier, the *Diaeta*[3].

11[1] – The word used in the original is niche : apsidal recess seems more appropriate.

11[2] – The reference to the side arcades is brought forward from the subsequent paragraph where it was obviously inserted to repair the omission made here.

11[3] – The U 273 A and U 314 A plans show that the central arcade was to stand between a pair of engaged columns abutted by half-pilasters. They also show that the outer side of the arcade would have been in line with the pilasters : consequently, the setting forward of the arcade would have equalled the protrusion of the pilasters.

11[4] – As remarked in Note 2 (2) *supra*, only the lower part of the road ever existed : it was never extended to reach the villa.

11[5] – Rome could only have been seen by looking right from the balustraded top of the portal.

12[1] – Hippodrome should certainly not be taken in the sense of a race track but in that of a place where horses might be assembled, exercised and eventually ridden in tournaments and other forms of pageantry.

12[2] – The length and width shown in the U 273 A plan are 82½ and 55 palmi.

13[1] – For the sake of clarity, the sequence of the enumeration has not been followed in the translation. The distribution is exactly as in the U 273 A plan. The adoption of the centralized plan entailed the suppression of this remarkable five-room suite.

13[2] – This would have been the only stairway providing a direct communication between the three levels of the villa. No equivalent exists in the U 314 A plan.

13[3] – As in the U 273 A plan, access to the portico of the walled-in garden is across the main level landing of the stairway linking the ground level with the attic storey. Horizontal and vertical transit movements would have

(13[3]) clashed at this point and, what is more, movements of two types of persons stepping at different paces : the occupants of the villa strolling leisurely to and fro, the members of the household going up and down the stairs. At a time, however, when officers and servants were in constant attendance the location of the stairway would not have seemed inconvenient.

14 – *Hora, tornando alla hoggia volta a greco, dalla banda verso maestro ha ne l'atro nichio una porta, a riscontro de l'atra che va nella sala descriptavi. Per questa s'entra in nun salotto largho 4 canne et lungho quanto la diagonale de suo quadrato con lli lumi medesimi volti a greco, con tre camere, doe che voltano a maestro et l'atra sopra il cortile tondo. Le due sono di proportione sexquitertia, camere da la state che mai haranno sole perché il monte gli tolli il ponente. Et queste riguardano una bella peschiera. Et de qui s'entra poi in una lhoggia, come V.S. intenderà.*

14 – We shall now go back to the North-East loggia. At its North-West extremity, in the other apsidal recess, is a doorway which corresponds to that of the hall we have just visited. Through it one enters a reception room, 4 *canne* wide and as long as the diagonal of a square formed with its width, which is lit from the North-East[1]. It is followed by three rooms, two facing North-West and one looking into the circular court[2]. The first two have a sesquitertial length to width relationship[3]. They are summer rooms where the sun cannot penetrate since the hill acts as a screen from the West. They overlook a fine fishpond. And Your Lordship will presently realize that from here one comes into yet another portico[4].

14[1] – A common point in the U 273 A and U 314 A plans is that the length of the hall is the same as the width plus the length of the twin rooms at the opposite end of the superstructure, plus the width of the wall separating the first from the second. Furthermore, the intention was obviously that the length of the second façade room should be the same as the width of the first minus the thickness of the wall. According to the text, the length of the hall was to have been 85 p. With a dividing wall of 4½ p., the width of the first room would thus have come to 42½ p., the length of the second to 38. The figure of 4 canne for the width of the first room must therefore be taken as an average. As to the diagonal of a 42½ p. square it is roughly 60 p.

14[2] – This is the first case in which the arrangement described is the same as in the U 314 A plan and the executed work. We shall meet another in the next paragraph. It follows that, when Raphael gave his description, he had already re-designed the NW half of the plan to accommodate the circular court. That he had yet to do the same for the other half is made abundantly clear by all that precedes.

14[3] – A sesquitertial ratio is a ratio of 4 to 3. With a length of 38 p., it produces a width of 28½. In the U 273 A and U 314 A plans alike, the length of the two rooms overlooking the fishpond is shown to be 38 p. whereas the widths are marked 28, except for the North angle room in the U 314 A plan where the width is 28½ p.

14[4] – Here again the word loggia has been translated as portico.

15 – Ho descripto a V.S. due porte nello cortile tondo, l'una che à la intrata da l'atrio, l'atra che entra in nella loggia volta a greco. Discontro alla porta de l'atrio ve n'è un'atra volta verso maestro, la quale intra in una bellissima lhoggia lungha 14 canne, la quale fa tre vani, et in quel del mezo è l'intrata. Gli atri doi hanno di riscontro un semicirculo che fanno spatiosa la lhoggia, tal che ha de vano 5 canne. Questa lhoggia verso il monte fa un semicirculo con li suoi sedili fatti a uso de pulmini. Et nel suo centro ha una bellissima fonte, et questa è una dietha da la stagione estiva molto delectevole perché non harà mai sole, et l'acque et c'è la verdura la fa bella.

15 – I have mentioned two portals in the circular court, those opening into the lobbies of the vestibule and of the North-East loggia. Opposite the first, on the North-West side of the court, another portal leads into a beautiful portico[1], 14 canne long, made up of three vaulted units of which the central is that one enters by. Each lateral unit is backed by an apsidal recess whereby its depth is brought up to 5 canne and the spaciousness of the portico is greatly increased[2]. At its hillside extremity, the portico forms a hemicycle with benches fashioned as cushioned seats[3]. In the centre is a very fine fountain[4]. The whole makes a delightful summer-time Diaeta since the sun never touches it and it is embellished by the sight of water and greenery[5].

16 – Da questa lhoggia si va in un xyxto, così chiamato da li antiqui, loco pieno d'arbori posti ad ordine, il quale xyxto è de lungheza et largheza del primo cortile, tal che questa villa è partita in tre, come V.S. ha inteso. Ha il xyxto certe sponde che guardano quatro canne et vede in quella baseza una peschiera lungha quanto il sito et largha cinquanta cinque palmi con certi gradi da sedervi et distendervi fino in fondo, e vi si viene dal sito con due larghe schale, una de chapo e l'atra da piè. Et in fine della schala volta a maestro ha a lato l'aqua una cenatione molto delectevole, la qual è per il fresco et per la veduta.

16 – Leaving the portico one enters an area such as the Ancients called Xystus[1]. Full of regularly planted trees it has the same length and width as the first court, thus giving the villa the tripartite division which Your Lordship will clearly perceive[2]. Bordered by a parapet, it overlooks a fishpond lying 4 canne below[3], the length of which is the same, with a width of 55 palmi[4]. Equipped with large steps to sit and stretch out on, the fishpond is reached from the Xystus[5] by two large stairways, one at each of its ends. And, at the bottom of the North-West stairway, by the water's edge, is a dining area made delightful by the scenery and prevailing coolness[6].

16[6] – In relation to the superstructure, the open-air dining area would therefore have been at the far end of the fishpond. There is no trace of such an area in the U 273 A plan, unless Raphael had in mind the platform at the foot of the stairways which is 14 p., or a little over 3 m., wide. In the U 314 A plan, suitable emplacements exist at both ends of the fishpond. On the other hand, the terminal stairways and the steps bordering the fishpond are features of the U 273 A plan. It looks as though Raphael, having revised the plan of the NW half of the superstructure, was in the process of doing the same for the fishpond area.

15[1] – See Note 9[1] sopra.
15[2] – In the U 273 A plan, the dimensions are the same as those of the NE loggia : 32 by 140 p. but, differing from the description, the plan shows no apsidal recesses. These belong in the U 314 A plan and in the executed work. In the reconstruction of the plan put into execution, the portico is 111 p. long and 33 p. wide. With apsidal recesses which are 16 1/2 p. deep, the total depth of the portico comes to 49 1/2 p.
15[3] – Benches fashioned as cushioned seats stand for pulmini which should be read Pulvini, a Latin word signifying cushions, pillows, cushioned seats.
15[4] – The U 273 A plan includes a fountain but no benches. The U 314 A plan and the executed work are devoid of both.
15[5] – See Note 7[1] sopra.

16[1] – Xystus is an Ancient Greek word designating a covered racing track in a gymnasium. In Rome, at the time of the Younger Pliny, it had come to mean a formally planted garden usually associated with a portico.
16[2] – In the U 273 A plan, the Xystus is made longer to compensate the fact that, in relation to its NW counterpart, the wing-encased SE façade is 45 p. farther away from the transversal axis of the villa. This results in the provision of a direct communication between the Xystus and the chapel described in the following paragraph. In the U 314 A plan, the lengths are the same.
16[3] – The implication is that the fishpond was to be level with the ground. In the executed work, it lies about 9 p. higher.
16[4] – This is the dimension shown in the U 273 A plan. In the same plan, the length of the fishpond is less than that of the Xystus by the width of the stairways about to be mentioned, plus that of the link with the chapel.
16[5] – From now on, in the original, the word sito is improperly used instead of Xyxtus.

27

17[1] – Properly speaking, this is not at the North angle of the Xystus but at that of the fishpond.

17[2] – See Note 7[2] sopra : the larger structure, with an internal diameter of 48 p., or 10.72 m., would have been better suited to such a destination.

17[3] – A circular bastion would have been utterly impossible here owing to the rise in the ground.

17[4] – Bulk of the villa is the term used instead of edifice since the latter is employed elsewhere to designate the superstructure.

18[1] – The U 273 A theatre is simpler than that about to be described. Though the plan does include an elaborately designed recess at the court level, the latter is not directly connected with the theatre. The U 314 A plan suggests an arrangement which is closer to that described.

19[1] – The system was clearly conceived as a one way ascending and descending circuit for ridden horses and mules, the length of each part amounting to some 550 p., or 123 m., not including the intermediary landings. The twice returned ramps, of which the lower would necessarily have been enclosed, could certainly not have provided a very exciting ride. Moreover, the doubling of the ramps at the back of the stage calling for a substantial increase in the depth of the area required at the orchestra level, the whole of the structure would have had to be lifted up the slope, well above the level of the U 314 A theatre, thus entailing a far from negligible ramp gradient. Finally, the height of the structure would have made it tower above the villa in a most unpleasant way.

[2] – Viterbo is on Via Cassia. Coming from there, about 7 kilometres before reaching the junction of Via Flaminia, one finds a road forking off to the right which climbs the North side of Monte Mario, passes at some distance behind the villa and goes winding

17 – *In capo del sito è un atro turrione, in l'angulo de tramontana, che acompagna quello della dietha dello inverno. Et sopra questo turrione vi è uno tempio tondo de l'alteza et largheza della dietha. Et questo serve per capella de questo loco. Similmente ne l'atro angulo del sito, apresso il monte v'è una bellissima porta che dà l'uscita al sito. Et questa è tutta la lungheza dello edifitio della villa.*

17 – At the North angle of the Xystus is a bastion similar to that of the winter Diaeta[1]. Atop stands a circular temple, of the same height and width as the Diaeta, which serves as a chapel[2]. Symmetrically, at the opposite end of the Xystus, is another bastion for defence purposes[3]. Between the two, a very fine portal leads out of the Xystus. And such is the bulk of the villa in the whole extent of its longitudinal development[4].

18 – *In lo cortile tondo ho scripto a V.S. tre porte : per l'una s'entra in una parte dello edifitio verso syroccho, per l'atra in la loggia a grecho, per l'atra a maestro dove è il sito. Hora resta la parte dello edifitio in verso il monte. In mezo, incontro alla porta della lhoggia de grecho, c'è uno spatio largho quanto è le schale che salghano al theatro del qual dirò poi. De riscontro a questa, di verso al monte, in tra le schale vi è una bella fonte et fa uno mezo circulo cavato nello monte, adornno de varii nichi marini et tartari d'aqua che fanno varii partimenti, secondo ch'è piaciuto allo arcfice, con lli sedili atornno. Et questa è un'atra dyetha, fatta per l'hora delli extremi caldi.*

18 – I have mentioned three portals in the circular court, those leading South-East toward the vestibule, North-East toward the loggia and North-West toward the Xystus. This leaves the part of the edifice built against the hill. In its centre, opposite the North-East portal, is a recess as deep as the width of the ramps leading up to the theatre about which I shall have more to say presently[1]. Hollowed out of the hillside, on a semi-circular plan, the recess contains a fine fountain. It is subdivided into compartments, decorated with sea-conchs and water accretions according to the contriver's fancy, and surrounded with benches. Here again we have a Diaeta, this time for the warmest hours of the day.

19 – *Da questa dietha da l'uno et l'atro lato, saliendo in verso syroccho et maestro con tre branche per lato, tanto comode che senza schalini e senza bastoni ve si va comodissimamente. Et in nel fine de l'una et de l'atra schala, nascie due atre branche che giunte insieme fanno un semicirculo. Et in nella loro coniuntione fanno una strada diritta a grecho et lybicco, la quale finicie de salire il monte e riecie alla strada de Monte Mario che viene da Viterbo a Roma, in modo che dalla strada de Monte Mario a quella de Ponte Molle vi è una strada diritta a corda et passa per mezo la villa apunto.*

19 – Of the ramps rising from the sides of this *Diaeta*, one heads North-West, the other South-East. Each is twice returned with a gradient so slight that neither steps nor half-billets are required. And from the top of these rise two more ramps forming together a semi-circumference[1]. They link up with a road continuing the ascent of the hill in a North-East/South-West direction, meeting the Monte Mario road from Viterbo to Rome and forming with the Ponte Milvio road a straight line passing through the centre of the villa[2].

28

20 – Hora in lo vano che resta piano tra le due schale che fanno il semicirculo, in questo spatio vi è un bello theatro fatto con questa misura et ragione : prima è fatto un circulo tanto grande se ha da fare il theatro, nel quale sono desegnati quatro trianguli esquilateri, li quali con le sue punte tochano le extreme linee del circulo. Et quel lato del triangulo che è volto a grecho et fa uno angulo a syroccho e l'atro a maestro, quello fa la fronte della scientia. Et da quel loco tirando una paralella per il centro de mezo, la quale separa et divide il pulpito del proscenio et la regione de l'horchestra, et così divisa et partita l'area sopra a queste misure, ce sono fatti lli gradi, la sciena, il pulpito et l'horchestra. Et de l'aquacede ce sono fatte le stantie dei scenici dove se habbitano a vestire, per non occupare la veduta del paese, il quale si serrerà solo con cose depinte quando se reciterano le comedie, acciò che la voce vadia alli spettatori. E questo theatro è collocato in modo che non può havere sole doppo il mezo di, la quale è hora solita a simili giochi.

20 – In the hemicycle formed by the twin upper ramps is a fine theatre planned as follows. First, a circumference is drawn, as large as the theatre, in which four equilateral triangles are inscribed with their tips touching the circumference. The base of the triangle turned toward the Greco (NE), the sides of which face the Sirocco (SE) and Maestrale (NW), is the Scaenae Frons[1]. Then a parallel is drawn through the centre of the circumference whereby the stage extrusion is separated from the orchestra and the limits of the stage and its extrusion, the orchestra and the steps of the auditorium are fixed[2]. Finally, the dressing-rooms are located where they do not interfere with the view[3]. Likewise, painted screens are used during performances to help carry the voices across to the audience[4]. And the way the theatre is placed makes it free from the sun in the afternoon, which is when it is normally used.

20[1] – Scaenae Frons, the wall backing the scene in the Ancient Roman theatres, is obviously what is meant by fronte della scientia. In the U 314 A plan, the wall is interrupted in its centre to afford a view beyond, an arrangement which is clearly implied in the text. As to the four triangles, the triangle terminating at the apex of the semi-circular wall which encloses the auditorium is not based on the Scaenae Frons but on the diameter of the orchestra edging the stage extrusion. In the present case, the three other triangles are irrelevant.

20[2] – Vitruvius gives a basic definition of the Roman theatre in Book V, Chapter VI. Raphael's description amounts to a sketchy summary of this definition. At the same time he departs from it in three important ways : by planning a theatre of which every single part may only be reached from the top of the auditorium, by providing the stage with a central extrusion – evidently inspired by Fra Giocondo's reconstruction of the Ancient Roman theatre – and by opening a big gap in the middle of the wall backing the stage.

20[3] – In the U 314 A plan, the dressing-rooms are placed in pairs at both ends of twin porticoes enframing the stage extrusion. This is another arrangement which is completely foreign to Ancient Roman practice.

20[4] – Regarding acoustics, painted screens could hardly have compensated the gap in the wall backing the stage. But the gap would have had the considerable merit of integrating the theatre with the rest of the villa. In this respect it might be added that the view from the top of the auditorium, in the U 314 A plan, would have been limited to the upper part of the circular court. There are two further observations to be made. They concern analogies. The first are those existing, in spite of certain differences, between the description and the U 314 A plan : they suggest that the design for the theatre was progressing in Raphael's mind simultaneously with the revision of the plans for the NW half of the superstructure and for the fishpond. The second observation proceeds from the analogy between Raphael's garden design for the villa, U 1356 A, and his conception of a fitting access for his theatre : the roundabout transit system of the first is reproduced, far less legitimately, in the second.

down toward the Vatican. This is the road referred to by Raphael. To reach it from the villa in the way indicated would have required a deep cutting across the hilltop.

22[1] – In the U 314 A plan, the dimensions of the hippodrome are shown as being 110 by 1044 p. while, in the U 273 A plan, they are roughly the same : the figure of 200 *canne* for the length of the hippodrome is therefore widely off the mark.

22[2] – Stables underlying the hippodrome may be the arrangement shown in the U 273 A plan. But it certainly is not that of the U 314 A plan in which the stables are faced with porticoes fronting the villa. On the other hand, a single level of stables could not provide more than 180 stalls or thereabouts : two levels would be needed to approach the figure of 400.

23[3] – In the same way as water is distributed throughout the U 273 A plan, within and without the superstructure.

23[1] – The observation as to the variety of *Cryptoportici* is very apt : it proves that Raphael had acquired a sound understanding of ancient Roman architecture.

21 – *E questo è tutto il piano de sopra. Et tutte le habitationi di questa villa sono de scoste dal monte per la sanità delli habitatori et tra le stantie e il monte vi sono lli cortili, come V.S. ha inteso. Questi cortili non sono in su le volte, ma sì bene l'habitationi et hanno sotto stanze alte quelle quatro canne che sono edeguamenti de l'alteza che un piano ha più che l'atro, come ho detto de sopra, le quali stanze di sotto sono dispense et ordinate come V.S. intenderà poi.*

21 – Such is the whole of the main storey. Your Lordship will understand that, for the well-being of the inhabitants, the living quarters are separated from the side of the hill by open courts which have no underlying accommodation. It follows that the lower level quarters are only to be found under those at the upper level, never under the courts. As I have said before, the difference in levels is 4 *canne*. And Your Lordship will soon be acquainted with the way in which the lower storey is distributed.

22 – *La via che viene da Ponte Molle et che fa intrata in mezo della villa, intra prima in lo hypodromo che è lungho 200 canne e largo 10. Questo hypodromo ha da un lato tutto lo edifitio per lungheza et da l'atro stalle per 400 cavalli, e queste stalle fanno argine et speroni a sostenere il piano e tutta la lungheza del hypodromo e lli cavalli volghano la testa a levante et greco come l'atro edifitio et posseli dare l'aqua per tutte le mangiatoie.*

22 – The road coming from Ponte Milvio toward the centre of the villa runs into the hippodrome. Measuring 200 by 10 canne, the latter is bounded on one side by the entire front of the villa[1]. On the other side are stables for 400 horses which are built in such a way as to abut and support the overlying hippodrome[2]. In the same way as the villa, the hippodrome looks to the East and North-East and so do the horses. And water may be distributed throughout the mangers[3].

23 – *Da lo hypodromo al diritto della strada de Ponte Molle è una bella porta doricha che, come ho detto, fa turrione. Et questa dà intrata del clytoportico cusì chiamato dalli antiqui. Et questo al nostro uso è uno portico sotteraneo, ancor che sono più sorte de clytoportico ma questo serve per vestibulo. A l'incontro della porta detta c'è un nichio con una fonte e de qua e de là trova due schale triangulare che montano in nel cortile e nella lhoggia volta a greco, come de sopra è detto.*

23 – On the axis of the Ponte Milvio road, there is a fine Doric portal which I have already described as a bastion. It leads into an area such as the Ancients called a *Cryptoporticus*. To us it is an underground portico. But bearing in mind that a *Cryptoporticus* could be of different types I should add that, in the present instance, it is a vestibule[1]. Opposite the entrance is an apse with a fountain at the sides of which are to be found the previously mentioned triangular stairways ascending to the court and North-East loggia.

24 – *Da man sinistra intrando in questo clytoportico in verso il mezo di se va nelli bagni dove anchora ve se può andare per lla schala secreta per lle parti de sopra, le quali sono così ordinate : hanno due camere da spogliarse et poi un loco tepido aperto da ungersi quando che uno se è bagnato et stufato. Et èvi la stufa calda et secca con lla sua temperatura et èvi lo bagno caldo con lli sedili da starvi secondo dove l'homo vole che l'aqua li bagni le parte del corpo. Et sotto la fenestra v'è un loco da porvisi a diacere e stare ne l'aqua ch'el servitore può lavare altrui senza farsi onbra. Di poi v'è un bagno tepido et poi un freddo, de tal grandeza che quando uno avesse voglia de volere notare, potria. Et la stantia di donde si schaldano questi lochi è accomodata con lla conserva e l'aqua et le caldare in modo dispensate, la fredda va nella tepida et la tepida nella calda, et quando se n'entra de l'una tanto ce ne ritornna de l'atra.*

24 – Having turned left on entering the *Cryptoporticus* and reached its southern extremity, one comes into the baths which are also accessible from the private stairway leading upward. And this is how the baths are arranged. First, there are two dressing-rooms followed by a tepid room in which to be anointed after having washed and taken the heat. Then comes a stove, hot and dry, a warm bath furnished with seats of varying heights according to which part of the body one wishes to clean and, in front of the window, a place where one may lie in the water and be washed by one's servant without coming under his shade. Finally, there are a tepid and a cold baths, the latter being large enough to swim in if one desires. The room where the heat is produced has its tanks and furnaces laid out in such a way that the cold water runs into the tepid, and the tepid into the warm, whatever flows into one coming out of the other[1].

25 – *Queste sono le stantie de una banda de' clytoportico. Da l'atra banda del clytoportico ci è la cucina secreta e le stanze per il quoco et una schala secreta da salire di sopra. Nella cima di questo edifitio, tra le volte e il tetto, v'è una alteza de due canne per lle habitationi della famiglia che è grandissima.*

25 – Such is the arrangement at one end of the Cryptoporticus. At the other end one finds the private kitchen, the cook's accommodation and a private stairway going up[1]. At the top of the superstructure, between the vaulting and the roof, are the living quarters of the household which is numerous. The height of the rooms is 2 canne.

26 – *V.S. può pensare che lli campi di questa villa sono habundanti de arbori, come si conviene a un talo edifitio; però non piglierò faticha de scrivere.*

26 – As Your Lordship may imagine, the grounds of the villa are covered with trees such as befit a residence of this type : but I shall spare myself the trouble of describing them.

24[1] – This part of the description brings further evidence as to Raphael's concern with comfort and practical matters. This concern – and his ability to meet its requirements – single him out among the architects of his time.

25[1] – The arrangement is exactly the same as in the executed work.

Appendix 2
Palmo subdivisions and metric equivalents

The unit of measurement used by Raphael was the palmo romano and its decuple, the canna. The palmo, worth 0.22342 metre, was subdivided into 12 oncie of 5 minuti each, or 60 minuti. In keeping with Cinquecento practice, the author follows the method of expressing dimensions in palmi and arithmetical fractions of the palmo.

Minuti	Oncie	Palmi	Metric	Minuti	Oncie	Palmi	Metric
1	$1/5$	$1/60$	0.00372	31	6 $1/5$		0.11543
2	$2/5$	$1/30$	0.00745	32	6 $2/5$	$8/15$	0.11916
3	$3/5$	$1/20$	0.01117	33	6 $3/5$		0.12288
4	$4/5$	$1/15$	0.01489	34	6 $4/5$		0.12660
5	1	$1/12$	0.01862	35	7	$7/12$	0.13033
6	1 $1/5$	$1/10$	0.02234	36	7 $1/5$	$3/5$	0.13405
7	1 $2/5$		0.02607	37	7 $2/5$		0.13778
8	1 $3/5$	$2/15$	0.02979	38	7 $3/5$		0.14150
9	1 $4/5$		0.03351	39	7 $4/5$		0.14522
10	2	$1/6$	0.03724	40	8	$2/3$	0.14895
11	2 $1/5$		0.04096	41	8 $1/5$		0.15267
12	2 $2/5$	$1/5$	0.04468	42	8 $2/5$		0.15639
13	2 $3/5$		0.04841	43	8 $3/5$		0.16012
14	2 $4/5$		0.05213	44	8 $4/5$	$11/15$	0.16384
15	3	$1/4$	0.05585	45	9	$3/4$	0.16756
16	3 $1/5$	$4/15$	0.05958	46	9 $1/5$		0.17129
17	3 $2/5$		0.06330	47	9 $2/5$		0.17501
18	3 $3/5$		0.06703	48	9 $3/5$	$4/5$	0.17874
19	3 $4/5$		0.07075	49	9 $4/5$		0.18246
20	4	$1/3$	0.07447	50	10	$5/6$	0.18618
21	4 $1/5$		0.07820	51	10 $1/5$		0.18991
22	4 $2/5$		0.08192	52	10 $2/5$	$13/15$	0.19363
23	4 $3/5$		0.08564	53	10 $3/5$		0.19735
24	4 $4/5$	$2/5$	0.08937	54	10 $4/5$		0.20108
25	5	$5/12$	0.09309	55	11	$11/12$	0.20480
26	5 $1/5$		0.09682	56	11 $1/5$	$14/15$	0.20852
27	5 $2/5$		0.10054	57	11 $2/5$		0.21225
28	5 $3/5$	$7/15$	0.10426	58	11 $3/5$		0.21597
29	5 $4/5$		0.10799	59	11 $4/5$		0.21970
30	6	$1/2$	0.11171	60	12	1	0.22342

Minuti	Oncie	Palmi	Metric	Minuti	Oncie	Palmi	Metric
90	18	1 $1/2$	0.33513	210	42	3 $1/2$	0.78197
120	24	2	0.44684	240	48	4	0.89368
150	30	2 $1/2$	0.55855	270	54	4 $1/2$	1.00539
180	36	3	0.67026	300	60	5	1.11710

*Illustrations
Section I:*

The villa as it stood in the 19th century

Fig. 1 Location plan

Detail from *Carta Topografica del Suburbano di Roma*, Filippo Trojani Inc., Roma, 1839

See paragraphs 5 and 6 and note 6 *supra**.

The orientation is North. At the bottom of the map, we can see the northern half of Rome showing Piazza Navona, Piazza del Popolo, Castel Sant'Angelo, the Borgo, St Peter's and the Vatican. Monte Mario is about half-way up, on the left, with the villa adhering to the North-East side of the hill.

* Paragraphs and notes are those in the Memoir
pages **9** to **21**.

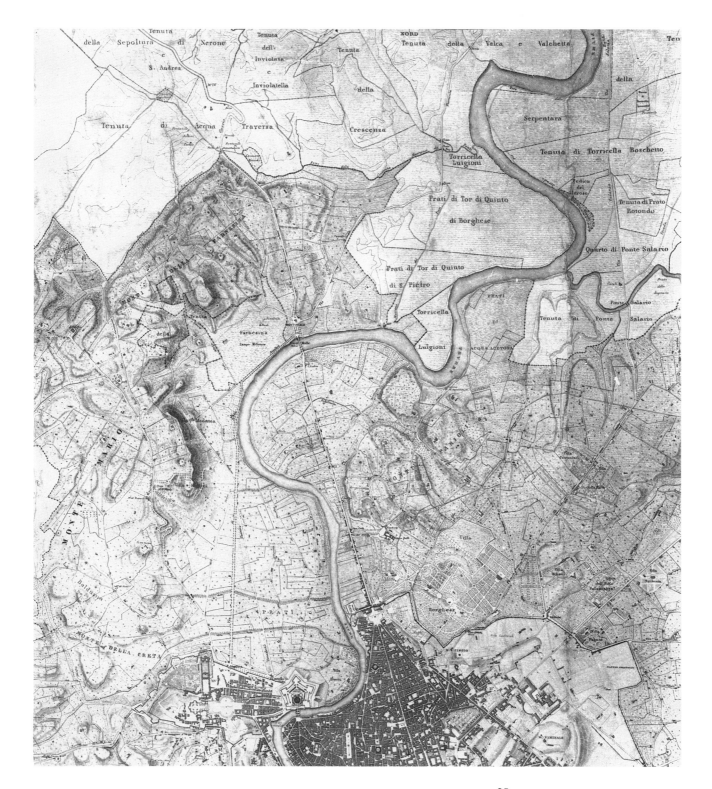

35

Fig. 2 H.J.E. Bénard: basement and superstructure plans

Paris, Bibliothèque de l'Ecole Nationale Supérieure des Beaux-Arts, Envois de Rome, 1871.

These plans, together with the elevations and cross-sections reproduced in figs 3 to 5 *infra*, show the villa very much as it looked when construction was abandoned some four and a half centuries ago. The basement plan was drawn to the scale of 1/200, the superstructure plan, the elevations and cross-sections were drawn to the scale of 1/100. Regarding orientation, the bottom part of the plans faces North-East.

From a functional point of view both plans may be divided into three main areas, a, b, c, the first providing horizontal and vertical means of communication throughout the building, the second accommodating the patron's private quarters and related dependencies, the third incorporating the open-air amenities set within the villa precinct. Considered independently, the various components of the plan are thus as follows.

At basement level: a) the executed part of the cryptoportico*, discussed in the commentary to Fig. 52, *infra*, backed by the stairwell discussed in paragraph 24 *supra*, b) the master kitchen, followed by the cook's room backed by a cellar, the latter showing an improvised access to the adjoining fishpond platform as part of the open-air dining arrangement discussed in paragraph 32 *supra*, c) the fishpond backed by the terrace-garden, the North-East front of the latter showing the plan of the waterside ambulatory.

At superstructure level: a) the executed part of the loggia, backed by the stairwell and the executed part of the circular court, the loggia being meant to connect the North-West part of the superstructure, which was built, to its South-East counterpart which was not, and the stairwell showing traces of the ruined, makeshift, stairway referred to in paragraph 24 *supra*, b) the terrace-garden portico, facing North-West, with its courtside lobby and the patron's apartment comprising three outward looking rooms plus two court-side rooms and, made accessible through the court-side rooms and their wall-embedded stairways, the four mezzanine rooms discussed in paragraphs 22 and 35 *supra*, c) the South-East terminations of the terrace-garden and fishpond, the latter showing the upper part of the fishpond stairway, the lower part of which may be seen in the basement plan.

* For this and other technical terms see Glossary, page 182.

36

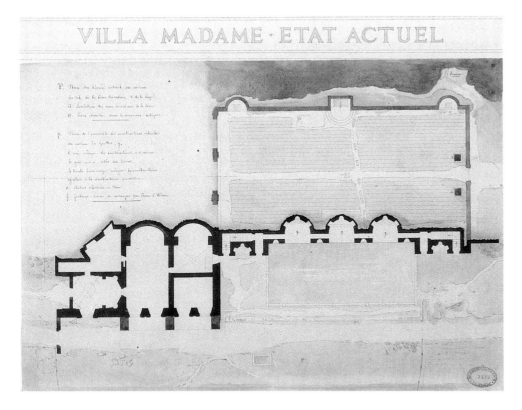

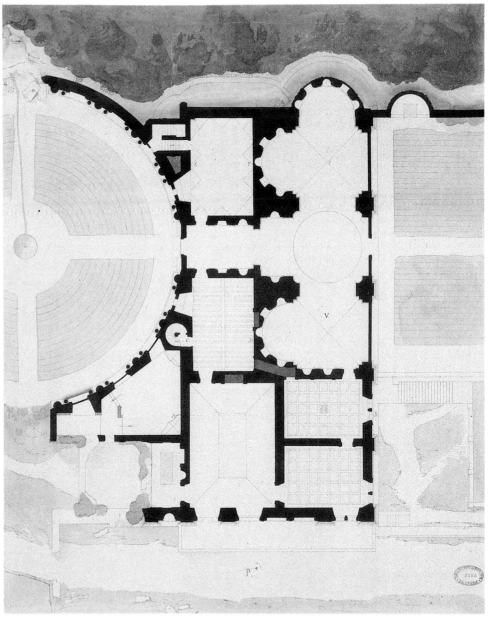

37

Fig. 3 H.J.E. Bénard: North-East front

Paris, Bibliothèque de l'Ecole Nationale Supérieure des Beaux-Arts, Envois de Rome, 1871.

The elevation displays several anomalies. The foremost lies in the presence of the twin-arched buttress referred to in paragraph 9 *supra*, another in the cross-window fenestration discussed in the same paragraph, yet another in the unbalanced character of the fishpond stairways considered in paragraph 32. In the left-hand part of the elevation may be seen the executed portion of the wall separating the loggia from the stairwell, the opposite side of which is the back of the circular court wall. The important detail of the loggia pilasters resting directly upon the pavement is mentioned in paragraph 9 *supra*.

VILLA MADAME · ETAT

ACTUEL ·

FAÇADE SUR LES JARDINS ·

Fig. 4 H.J.E. Bénard: cross-section at superstructure level

Paris, Bibliothèque de l'Ecole Nationale Supérieure des Beaux-Arts, Envois de Rome, 1871.

In the upper drawing, the cross-section adheres to the longitudinal axis of the villa. It shows that the main order pedestal applies throughout and that, in the circular court, the top of the superimposed pedestal runs even with the top of the lower tier in the pilastered bays of the lobby and North-West portico. It also shows that the domed vault, at the center of the portico, causes a surelevation of the attic floor. Another interesting detail is that of the frieze-enclosed window, in the façade. Placed at 1 $\frac{1}{3}$ palmi, or 2.30 metres, above the floor level it signifies that adequate living quarters were only to be found overlooking the court, the rest of the accommodation consisting of mere garrets. Lastly, in the lower drawing, may be seen the compound rib-vaulting mentioned in paragraph 9 *supra*.

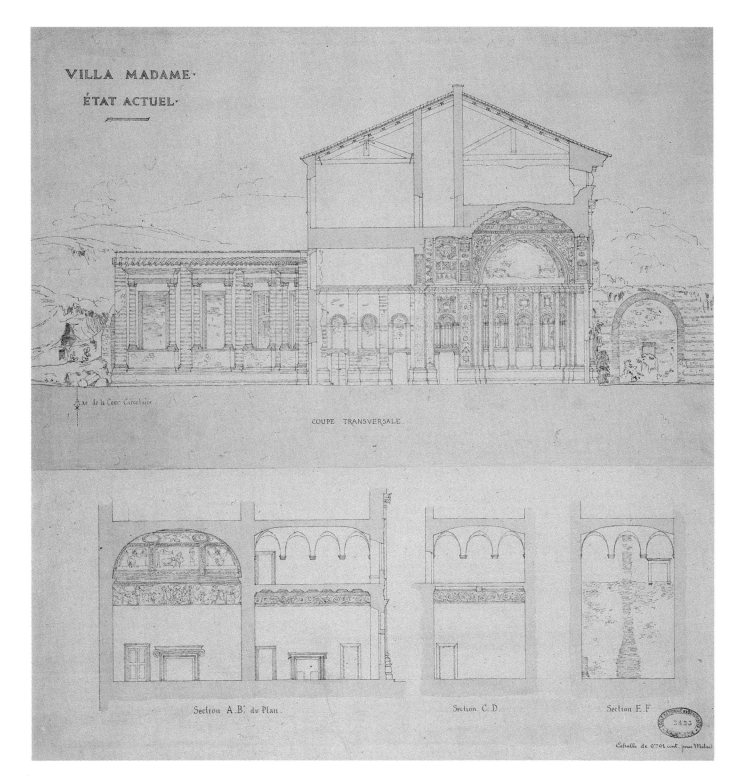

VILLA MADAME·

ÉTAT ACTUEL·

Axe de la Cour Circulaire.

COUPE TRANSVERSALE.

Section A.B. du Plan.

Section C.D.

Section E.F.

Échelle de 0.01 cent. pour Mètre.

See paragraphs 10, 27 to 29 *supra*, figs 46, 47 and 48 *infra*.

Devoid of its stucco coating and decorations, deprived of the transitive effect of its arcades, the façade inadequately reflects the merits of its design. Yet, thanks to the fullness of its proportions and the appropriateness of its order, it unquestionably answers the purpose of irradiating a lush serenity. As we have seen it has its faults. Regarding the windowed part of the elevation there are two reasons why the median pilaster is objectionable. One comes from its analogy with an isolated support blocking a passage, the other from an interspacing of the pilasters which is closer in the windowed than in the arcaded part. The windows themselves are equally objectionable and their presence together with that of the pilaster, can only be explained through the circumstances prevailing at the time of their implementation. When it became imperative to solve the problems posed by an eventual adaptation of the Pantheon-type window, and the re-arrangement of the windowed part of the elevation, there must have been growing misgivings in Raphael's mind as to the completion of the villa. It is therefore highly probable that he entrusted Giulio Romano with the task at hand, the latter using the commitment to assert himself by adopting expeditive solutions in complete opposition with the general design. As a justification he may well have invoked the pretext of investing the villa with a rusticity befitting its location. Indeed, Raphael himself gave a remarkable example of architectural expressionism with the design of the terrace-garden gateway reproduced in Fig. 15 *infra*. But in a case such as this, where the effect produced does nothing but impair the fulsome elegance of the elevations, a pretence to expressionism would merely have served as an excuse for facility. The perversity of the median pilaster is best seen in Fig. 12 *infra*, the offensiveness of the window in Fig. 22.

An interesting arrangement is to be observed at the West end of the building where the angular effect is neutralized through the collocation of independently returned pilasters. The same arrangement may be seen in the North corner of the superstructure, in the U 273 A plan.

The cross-section of the fishpond passes by the middle of an apsidal recess. The arched passage through the sidewall is part of the waterside ambulatory shown in plan form, in Fig. 2 *supra*. To be noted is the water penetration under the vault-supported pavement of the recess. Common to the three recesses, the disposition is clearly shown in Fig. 11 *infra*.

VILLA MADAME.

ETAT ACTUEL.

FAÇADE DU CÔTÉ

de la LOGE.

Echelle de 0^m.01 pour mètre.

43

Fig. 6 General view from the East

Brogi negative no. 1843
Florence, Archivi Alinari

See paragraph 9.

On the left, projecting from the sunlit side of the superstructure facing South-East, the following components appear clearly: the executed part of the circular court, the triangular stairwell rising from the basement, at the side of which ascends the turret enclosing the provisional stairway serving the mezzanine and attic storeys, and finally the executed part of the North-East loggia with its niche-bearing end-wall. Further right is the North-East front of the superstructure, overlying the addititious twin-arched buttress, followed by the back wall of the fishpond surmounted by the terrace-garden gateway. Had the rest of the project been executed, a superstructure unit of the same size as the first would have been built on the opposite side of the completed circular court, the two units being reunited by means of the completed loggia and concurring to form with the latter a monumental North-East façade surmounting the basement . Likewise, the basement would have been extended to occupy, at the South-East end of the completed superstructure, an area of the same size and shape as that occupied by the terrace-garden and fishpond at its North-West side, this for the purpose of incorporating an entrance court, a walled-in garden and some additional accommodation. The planned theatre would have been sunk into the hill-side, at the back of the circular court, while two long ranges of stabling were to be built, facing the North-East front of the complex, at a distance of 110 palmi or slightly less than 25 metres.

Fig. 7 Executed part of the circular court

Anderson negative no 17702
Original slide destroyed

See paragraph 24, figs 2 and 4 *supra*, plus figs 25, 31, 32 and 51 *infra*.

The court enclosure is tangential to the South-East wall of the superstructure as it would have been to its return, at the back of the North-East loggia. Where it lines the hill-side, on the contrary, it extends beyond the South-West end of the superstructure and penetrates a coomb into which, at a higher level, the theatre should have been inserted. Going by the size of its engaged columns, the height of the main order would have been such as to make the top of its crowning parapet run even with that of the string-course underlying the attic-storey windows. Had the villa been completed, therefore, the upper part of the twice returned superstructure walls would have appeared as partly encasing the circular court enclosure, thereby forming triangular-like platforms in the superstructure corners but leaving, at the side of the hill, an open terrace surmounted by the back of the stage building. At the right of the attic-storey windows may be seen a walled-in arched opening which corresponds with the attic-storey corridor planned to serve the three sides of the superstructure: the ultimate flight of the returned stairway, mentioned in paragraph 24 would naturally have been in line with this opening. The order of the court enclosure is discussed in the commentaries to Figs 25, 31 32 and 51 *infra*. Obliterated in the course of renovation, the end-wall of the North-East loggia is reconstructed in Fig. 49.

Fig. 8 Prospect of the Sabina countryside

Brogi negative no 020
Whereabouts unknown

See paragraph 6 *supra.*

View taken at the end of the nineteenth century. It shows Ponte Milvio, in the centre of the picture, and the tree-lined riverside road leading to the North end of the bridge. Owing to the clouds and haze the distant rise in the land is not discernible: it is in the N.D. Boguet drawing reproduced next.

Fig. 9 Nicolas-Didier Boguet: The Tiber Valley

Rome, Gabinetto Nazionale delle Stampe, F.N. 5658

The view-point must have been just off the drive leading to the villa, about half-way up. It gives a better idea of the landscape than does Fig. 8. Showing Ponte Milvio with its northern gateway as reconstructed by Valadier, in 1805, the drawing may have been made in the years 1813-1815.

Fig. 10 General view from the North

Moscioni negative
Musei Vaticani, Archivio Fotografico, VI-3-8

See paragraphs 8, 9, and 10 *supra*.

The North-East end of the superstructure should be considered in relation with Fig. 3 *supra*, the unsuitability of the superstructure windows appearing more clearly in the present photograph than in the Bénard drawing. At basement level, the additititious character of the twin-arched buttress is manifest. In the North-West façade, the portico standing at the head of the terrace-garden justifies Raphael's use of the word 'xystus' to describe the latter: see Appendix 1, 16, Note 1. To realize how enclosed the garden would have been one should imagine the South-West and North-West walls brought up to their proper height, about 2 metres above their present level, and the North-West wall continued across the whole width of the fishpond to link up with the planned North tower.

Fig. 11 Fishpond and terrace-garden from the East

Anderson negative no 17703
Florence, Archivi Alinari

This photograph is more than a simple document. Presenting a poignant image of forsaken grandeur, it is a remarkable specimen of the photographer's art. Among the three Anderson pictures included in this series, it is the only one that may still be reproduced from an original print, the slides of the two others having been either broken or destroyed.

The apsidal recesses, the waterside ambulatory and the fishpond stairways are discussed in the commentaries to figs 19, 20 and 21. The underwater recesses, referred to in the commentary accompanying Fig. 5, were most probably meant to collect the water issuing from the fountains in the apsidal recesses. Alternatively, they could have served as fish-havens.

At the level of the terrace-garden, the big niche on the left occupies the centre of the wall skirting the hillside. It was decorated by Giovanni da Udine and contains a fountain featuring the famous elephant head modelled after that of Annone, the white elephant presented to Pope Leo X, in 1514, by the King of Portugal. At the far end of the garden, sparkling in the morning sun, is the gateway reproduced in Fig. 15.

Returning to the fishpond level, there is a good opportunity to appreciate the soundness of the opinion expressed in paragraph 33, as to the inadequate width of the stairway extrusion. This inadequacy is all the more striking if one considers that the platform upon which the present extrusion was to stand would have been lined, on its North-West side, by a return of the basement wall surmounted by a continuation of the garden wall, both extending as far as the North tower: see Fig. 44.

Fig. 12 Superstructure from the North-West

Moscioni negative
Musei Vaticani, Archivio Fotografico, VI-3-11

See paragraphs 10 and 11, plus figs 5 and 46 to 48.

Fig. 13 Main order capital and entablature

Moscioni negative
Musei Vaticani, Archivio Fotografico: VI-3-13

See Th. Hofmann, op.cit. *note 9 supra*, which contains measured drawings of most architectural details. The entablature comes from Pl. XXXIX, the capital from Pl. XL. (overleaf).

The design of the capital comes from an antique Roman derivation of the Ionic, a late example of which may be seen in the Temple of Saturn, at the foot of the Capitol, in the Forum Romanum. In Renaissance Rome a few such capitals pre-date the present one, such as in the Edicola di S. Andrea, Cimitero dei Pellegrini, built by Francesco del Borgo, in 1462. The volutes are comparatively small, angled and unattached, their fillet springing directly from the abacus. The latter rests directly on the echinus and the customary fillet-cum-astragal underlying the echinus is replaced by fasciae. Taken from the astragal topping the shaft of the pilaster, the height of the capital is 0.708 metres or 3 $\frac{1}{6}$ palmi.

The module of the order – which is taken here as half the thickness of the column or pilaster – is 3 palmi or 180 minuti. On converting Hofmann's metric measurements it appears that the total height of the entablature comes so close to 13 $\frac{1}{2}$ palmi, or 4 $\frac{1}{2}$ times the module, as to make it certain that such was the intended dimension. It puts the height of the architrave at 4 $\frac{1}{3}$ palmi, that of the pulvinated frieze at 4 and that of the cornice at 5 $\frac{1}{6}$ or, in terms of a subdivision of the module into 18 parts of 10 minuti, or 2 oncie, at 26, 24 and 31 parts respectively. The protrusion of the entablature is 4 $\frac{5}{6}$ palmi or 29 parts of the module. The main difference with the usual Ionic entablature lies in the substitution of modillions to dentils under the corona.

Capital and entablature stand out as a most felicitous piece of Composite design. In Fig. 23, we shall see that the base and pedestal are equally remarkable: altogether the order is one of the finest produced in the Cinquecento.

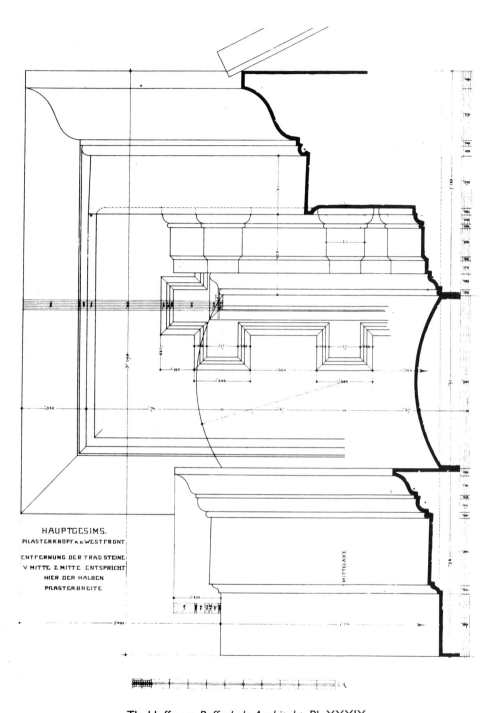

HAUPTGESIMS.
PILASTERKROPF a. WESTFRONT

ENTFERNUNG DER TRAGSTEINE
V. MITTE Z. MITTE ENTSPRICHT
HIER DER HALBEN
PILASTERBREITE

MITTELAXE

Th. Hoffman: *Raffael als Architekt*, Pl. XXXIX

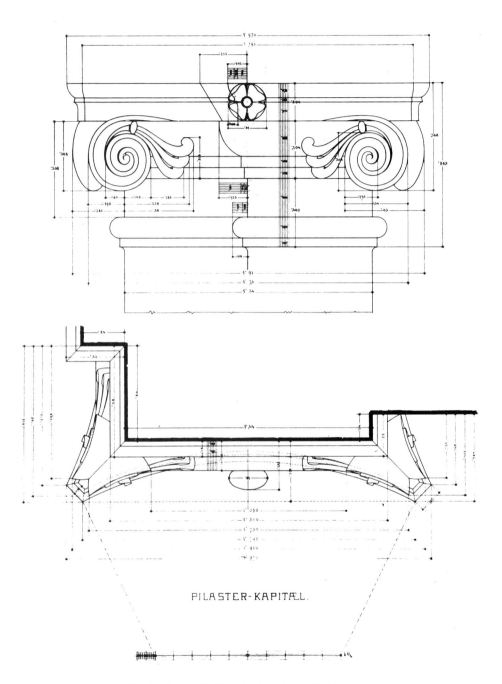

PILASTER-KAPITÆL.

Th. Hoffman: *Raffael als Architekt*, Pl. XL

Fig. 14 Interior of North-West portico

Anderson negative no 17704
Florence, Archivi Alinari, original slide now broken

See reconstructed plan in Fig. 41, elevation of end wall in Fig. 49 and isometric perspective in Fig. 50.

Responding to the openness of the garden arcades, the curvature of the apsidal recesses and the deepness of the central lobby are determining factors of spatial fluidity. The wall separating the portico from the ensuing apartment does not only fulfill a practical purpose. In relation with the South-West wall of the terrace-garden, it emphasizes the general centrality of the axis passing by the middle of the lobby. It also increases the amplitude of the adjoining apsidal recess and, above all, it serves as a background to the phenomenon occurring, at the opposite end of the portico, where the returned recesses give the impression of being diagonally juxtaposed. Indeed, owing to the semi-interred character of the area, it looks as though these recesses had been built within a hill-side cavern, the slanting axis of the juxtaposition coinciding with the bisecting line of the cavern. Suggesting a compliance with environmental circumstances, the integration effect is all the more spectacular since the axis of the juxtaposition and the longitudinal axis of the portico naturally intersect at the centre of the related portico compartment.

The extremely rich and diversified decoration of the portico was executed in the years 1520-1523, largely no doubt after Raphael's designs. The main contributors were Giulio Romano and Giovanni da Udine and, to a lesser extent, Baldassare Peruzzi and Giovan Francesco Penni. There is unfortunately no recent discussion of the work.

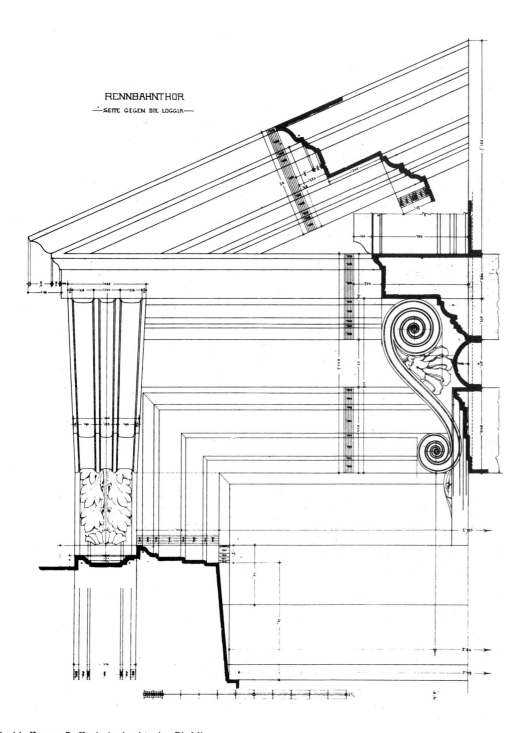

RENNBAHNTHOR
—SEITE GEGEN DIE LOGGIA—

Th. Hoffman: *Raffael als Architekt*, Pl. XL

Fig. 15 Gateway concluding the terrace-garden

Musei Vaticani, Archivio Fotografico: VI-3-12
Th. Hofmann, *op. cit. note 9 supra*, Pl. XL.

Straddling the passage from the protected precinct of the villa into the outer grounds, incorporating a number of elements unconventionally dimensioned, the sturdy gateway clearly stands to reconcile Apollonian harmony with Dionysian unruliness thereby exalting its function as an intermedium between inner and outer spaces. Indeed, it is a masterpiece of expressionist architecture. The work has been ascribed to Giulio Romano but the elegance of its design, the refinement of its details, leave no room for doubt as to Raphael's authorship. The wooden door-leaves no longer exist: the grille surmounting them recalls the balustrading in Raphael's Vatican loggia.

The height of the entablature is 1.25 metres equal to 5 ³/₄ palmi and the thickness of the architraved surround is 0.445 metres or 2 palmi. Going by the proportions of the superstructure entablature, the height of the pulvinated frieze should be around 1 ⁵/₆ palmi and that of the cornice around 2 ⁵/₁₂, the total coming to 6 ¹/₄ palmi instead of 5 ³/₄, the height of the frieze having been brought down to 1 ¹/₆ palmi and that of the cornice up to 2 ⁷/₁₂. The crushing of the frieze naturally makes the consoles supporting the corona quite bulky, added to which the corona itself is thicker than it should normally be. It follows that the reduced height of the whole entablature gives the architraved part of the surround a visual impact which equals that of the oversized corona and binds both elements, plus the diminutive frieze, into one solid mass of overhanging stonework. The pitch in the pediment is 22 ¹/₂ degrees. The colossal statues at the sides of the gateway are by Baccio Bandinelli (1493-1560).

Illustrations Section 2:

The villa as it stands to-day

Fig. 16 General view from the air – 1

Fotocielo negative

Original prints having proved unobtainable, this view and that reproduced in Fig. 17 have been taken from *Roma del Rinascimento*, by Paolo Portoghesi, Venice, 1970.

See paragraph 10 *supra*.

Fig. 17 General view from the air

Fotocielo negative: see commentary to Fig. 16 *supra*.

See paragraph 10 *supra*.

  Notwithstanding the fuzziness of the image one may see the columnated adjunction to the superstructure façade, the decorative arcade at the back of the terrace surmounting it and, on either side of the radiating arcade and in the windowed bays of the North-West façade, the openings cut into the frieze underlying the entablature.

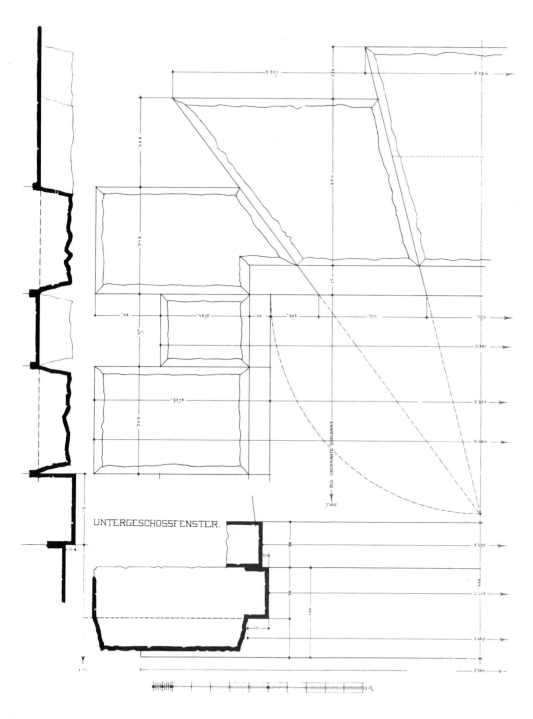

Th. Hoffman: *Raffael als Architekt*, Pl. XXXVII

Fig. 18 Basement window

Vasari negative
Paris, GD
Th. Hofmann, *op. cit. note 9 supra*, Pl. XXXVII.

This design has been a source of inspiration for architects all over Europe, up to the very end of classicism.

The window aperture averages 2.235 by 3.65 metres or 10 by 16 ½ palmi.

With a protrusion of 0.165 metres equal to ¾ palmi or thereabouts, the rusticated quoins average alternating heights of 0.370 and 0.550 metres which dimensions are so close to 1 ⅔ and 2 ½ palmi – the relationship being 2 to 3 – as to suggest that such were the intended ones. Since there are four courses of each to a jamb the implication is that the height of the aperture should be 16 ⅔ palmi, rather than 16 ½, thus producing a width to height relationship of 3 to 5. The wedge-shaped quoins in the lintel are cut at angles of 52 and 75 degrees originating from a median point 5 palmi below the underside of the lintel.

Fig. 19 Fishpond from the East

Vasari negative
Paris, GD

See paragraph 32, Appendix 1, 16, figs. 2, 3, 5 and 11 *supra*, plus figs. 43 and 44 *infra*.

We have seen that Raphael initially thought of the fishpond as lying at the foot of a series of steps whereby, to use his own words, the waterside might be reached to sit or recline by. The executed work is a very different proposition. Set at a higher level, the pond is enclosed within a parapet which merely invites circumambulation. In fact, with its back-wall featuring three grotto-like apsidal recesses, probably meant to house an elaborate system of fountains, the fishpond is very much akin to an antique nymphaeum.

We have also seen that the planned length of the fishpond platform was 235 palmi The dimension being divisible into five parts of 47 palmi, of which one was given to the width of each platform end and the other three to the length of the pond, the latter should come to 141 palmi, with a width of 52, the actual dimensions being practically the same.

Corresponding to 117 layers of $1/4$ palmo thick brick courses, the back-wall is $32\,1/4$ palmi high which means that the platform lies $9\,3/4$ palmi above ground level. The quality of the brickwork is good and makes it likely that it was to remain apparent. The three apsidal recesses alternate with four raised niches. Unlike the other arches in the villa those of the apsidal recesses are neither stilted, nor made to look so as in the radiating arcade of the North-East façade. Going by the Elephant Fountain of the terrace-garden, to be seen in the upper left part of Fig. 11 *supra*, it is practically certain that the archivolts of the niches and apsidal recesses were to be stuccoed.

Fig. 20 Waterside ambulatory

Vasari negative
Paris GD

See figs. 2 and 11 *supra*, 43 and 44 *infra*.

The centre of curvature of the apsidal recesses is set back 9 palmi whereas the width of the arched openings interconnecting the recesses is 5 1/4 palmi and the thickness of the façade wall is 3 3/4 palmi The inner side of the openings is therefore in line with the centre of curvature of the recesses which means that the inner part of their archivolt would have been slightly bent, thus harmonizing with the surrounds of the rectangular niches and the archivolt of the central niche. Owing to the repetitive character of the apsidal recesses it is probable that the fountains would have been confined within the niches and associated with semi-circular benches. The relatively enormous expanse of the vaults makes it unlikely that they were to be decorated in any other way than with a stucco revetment imitating water accretions. Since the raised niches outside would certainly have contained fountains as well, walking down the ambulatory should have procured the sensation of passing through an uninterrupted outpouring of water adroitly controlled.

Fig. 21 Fishpond stairway

Vasari negative
Paris, GD

See paragraph 32 and figs 2, 3 and 5 *supra*, plus 43 and 44 *infra*.

Having cast aspersions at the fishpond stairways for being at odds with the rest of the design, the author shall now consider them as separate entities. Evolved as they were to meet practical requirements of a trivial nature, it is a fact that they unexpectedly took on such a character as to make them figure prominently among examples of make-believe garden architecture. Indeed, leading down to a wall-backed hanging platform from where the only way out is by means of an earthborn doorway, the exposed part of the stairways definitely evokes the passage from one world into another, the impression being enhanced by the constricted and seemingly haphazard location of the doorway which suggests a subordination to unnatural contingencies. Having thus trapped one to sink into darkness, the obliterative process turns redemptive by bringing one back to light, at the bottom of the immured part of the stairways, and giving one access to the beautiful surroundings devised by Raphael which, under the circumstances, might be considered as emblematic of a felicitous afterlife. In short, whatever the reasons that make them look the way they do, the stairways are highly effective as reverie-inspiring items of architectural design. Moreover, in the face of Cardinal Giulio's open-air dining fancy, it must be admitted that the façade of the stairway extrusions afforded a better background to ecclesiastical conviviality than outwardly returned flights of steps. Such were certainly the arguments put before Raphael to vindicate the solution adopted.

Fig. 22 Superstructure window

Vasari negative
Paris, GD

See paragraphs 9, 28, 29, plus note 11 *supra*.

The aperture is 2.235 by 3.725 metres or 10 by 16 ⅔ palmi. With a width of 0.445 metres or 2 palmi, which is only five times less than the width of the aperture, the surround reaches the dimensions of 14 by 18 ⅔ palmi. Consequently, the unusually wide window is unusually low, the width to height relationship being 3 to 5 for the aperture, 3 to 4 for the surround. The mullioning and transoming does not improve matters. It makes the window look paltry in comparison with the basement windows which are exactly the same size. It also breaks the balance of proportions between the surround and the aperture, the fractioning of the second making the first look largely over-dimensioned. The fact that the device was adopted after the window had been set in shows in the joinery: had the mullion and transom been part of the original structure, their outer ends would have been incorporated into the surround, the joints cutting across the whole width of the latter.

The cornice has a height of 0.335 or 1 ½ palmi and a protrusion of 0.270 metres or 1 ⅕ palmi. Designed in the manner of an impost, it consists of an ogeed corona supported by a cymatium which rests directly upon the surround. Infringing upon the constricted area comprised between the top of the window surround and the underside of the main string-course, the cornice is unduly low. But the cymatium protrudes so strongly – by ⅘ ths of its height – and the ogee overlying the corona is so powerful that the strong shadows cast are in keeping with the importance of the surround. To a certain extent, therefore, the inadequate height of the cornice is compensated by its profile. Here again one must imagine the motif with its stucco coating.

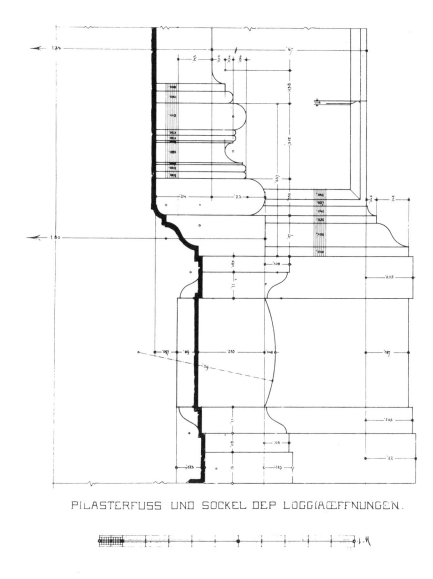

PILASTERFUSS UND SOCKEL DEP LOGGIAŒFFNUNGEN.

Fig. 23 Main order pedestal and base

Vasari negative
Paris, GD
Th. Hofmann, *op. cit. note 9 supra*: Pl. XXXVIII

See figs 3, 5 and 12 *supra*.

The pedestal runs around the entire superstructure, including the circular court, the North-East loggia and the North-West portico. Where the pedestal is brought forward to support the main order pilasters, its otherwise flat die is pulvinated. Where it supports the pillars of the radiating arcade, in the North-East façade, the die is unpulvinated. The height of the pedestal is given by Hofmann as being 0.945 to 0.960 whereas, in fact, it has been found to vary between figures which are slightly under the first and slightly over the second. The chances are that it was meant to be 9.57 metres or 4 $1/3$ palmi, after having first been made 4 $1/2$ palmi and reduced when the dimensions of the elevation were finally decided upon. The protrusion of the fillet capping the top ogee is the same as that of the upper plinth fascia. It is $1/2$ palmo, while the lower fascia protrudes another $1/12$ palmo to reach $7/12$ palmo.

The base is in keeping with the simplified Composite character of the order. It includes thin double tori at the edges of the scotia and a supplementary torus under the shaft. The height of the base, minus the shaft fillet, is equal to the module of 3 palmi. Vertically it is divided into three parts, one of 1 $2/5$ palmi being made up of the plinth and lower torus, another, of the same 1 $2/5$ palmi, being made up of the scotia and upper torus while the third, of $1/5$ palmo, comprises a complementary torus.

The shaft of the pilasters, including its bottom fillet and top fillet-cum-astragal, turns out to be 10.612 metres or 47 $1/2$ palmi high, thereby leaving 0.708 metres or 3 $1/6$ palmi for the height of the capital.

Fig. 24 Doric capital and Composite impost

Vasari negative
Paris, GD

See page 86 and figs 48 and 58 *infra*.

In the twin-level garden, at the South-East end of the villa, the pieces serve as socles to large flowerpots. They include two Doric capitals, one Composite impost and a number of Tuscan bases, all fashioned to the same half-diameter module of 1 ⁴/₅ palmi, or 108 minuti, divisible into 18 parts of 6 minuti. As we shall see, the size of the capitals perfectly fits the requirements of the loggia screen columns. But the Composite impost hardly seems to apply, the number of bases largely exceeds the four required and the height of their plinth suggests that they should be partly sunk into the ground. It is probable, therefore, that all these pieces were meant to form part of a free-standing garden colonnade set between two impost-surmounted square pillars. This is all the more likely since the pieces are in granite, not in travertine.

Nonetheless, the capitals and the bases, the latter with a normalized plinth, have been used in the reconstruction of the design. With a module of 108 minuti, the height of the loggia columns, being 27 palmi , or 1620 minuti, turns out to be the standard dimension of 15 times the module. The height of the capital is also equal to the standard module plus one part, that is 114 minuti. It is made up of 36 minuti for the neck, 3 times 5 minuti for the overlying fillets, 21 minuti each for the echinus and abacus, 15 minuti for the surmounting ogee and 6 minuti for the thickness of the tablet. The neck of the capital has a half-diameter of 96 minuti, which means that the diminution would have amounted to 12 minuti or 2 parts, which is slightly less than average. The total protrusion of the capital amounts to 4 minuti in relation to the upper part of the shaft, 36 minuti in relation to its lower part. As for the base, the height of its plinth has been brought down from 80 to 62 minuti, thereby making its lower torus, which is 30 minuti thick, coincide with the prolongation of the lower ogee in the pedestal of the main order. The upper torus being 16 minuti thick gives the base the standard height of 1 module or 108 minuti whereas, in relation to the bottom of the shaft, its protrusion is only 30 minuti, or 5 parts, thereby making it particularly suitable for the intercolumnar insertion of balusters.

The impost comprises two fasciae enclosing an ogee and surmounted by a torus supporting a cyma topped by a fillet underlying the tablet. In plan, the lower fascia is 198 minuti square, its sides being therefore 6 minuti, or 1 part, longer than the neck diameter of 192 minuti.

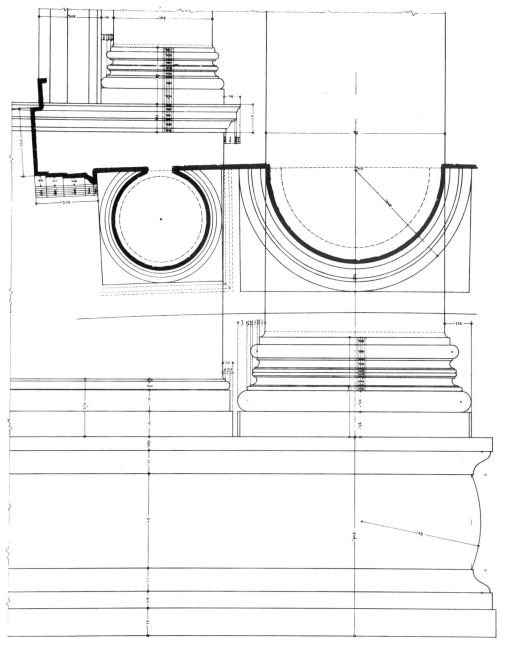

ARCHITEKTUR VOM RUNDHOFE.

Fig. 25 Circular court pedestals and column bases

Vasari negative
Paris, GD
Th. Hofmann, *op. cit. note 9 supra*, Pl. XXXIX

See figs 2, 4, 6, 7 *supra*, and 32, 44 and 51 *infra*: Fig. 7 gives a general view of the uncompleted circular court, the commentary to Fig. 44 contains the essential dimensions, together with the specifications regarding the setting of the columns, and Fig. 51 shows a tentative reconstruction of the complete ordonnance.

The elevation detail, reproduced in the present photograph and in the Hofmann drawing, is yet another unadulterated example of Raphael's exceptional designing ability. We have already seen that the lower pedestal is the same as in all the other parts of the superstructure and that the superimposed pedestals, supporting the aedicular windows, reach the same height as the lower tier cornices in the North-West portico and North-East loggia, to wit 11 ¼ palmi from the ground up. The half-diameter modules of the columns are respectively 2 and 1 ¹/₁₀ palmi, or 120 and 66 minuti. In both cases the bases are one module high, divided into two equal parts, the lower comprising the plinth and main torus, the upper, two superimposed scotiae surmounted by the secondary torus. Their composition is the same as that of the Pantheon Corinthian bases, but with slightly different proportions. Another difference is that they protrude much less owing, no doubt, to the insetting of the first and the presence of the window surrounds in the case of the second, the protrusions being 36 and 16 minuti respectively. The rest of the ordonnance is discussed in the commentary to Fig. 51.

Illustrations Section 3:

Sources of inspiration, original plans, elevations and related documents

Fig. 26 Rome, Basilica of Constantine, North-West transept

Vasari negative
Paris, GD

The Basilica was started under Maxentius and finished under Constantine, in the early 4th century AD. In Raphael's day, its remains were the most impressive in the Campo Vaccino, the site of the dilapidated Forum Romanum where, ever since the return of the Papacy from Avignon towards the end of the 14th century, the ancient monuments were being actively quarried out. There cannot be much doubt that it was from this example of a vault-enclosed threefold fenestration system that Raphael evolved his scheme for the main hall of the villa and the radiating arcades of the North-East facade.

Fig. 27 Gianfrancesco da Sangallo: plan of Raphael's early project

Florence, Galleria degli Uffizi, Gabinetto dei Disegni e delle Stampe, no. 273 A, detail

See paragraphs 13 to 18 *supra* and figs 52 to 56 *infra*.

We know that the plan was executed, by Gianfrancesco da Sangallo, in the summer months of 1518: see C.L. Frommel in *op. cit. note* 20, p. 326, 2. 16. 3. Construction of the cryptoportico was started in accordance with this plan.

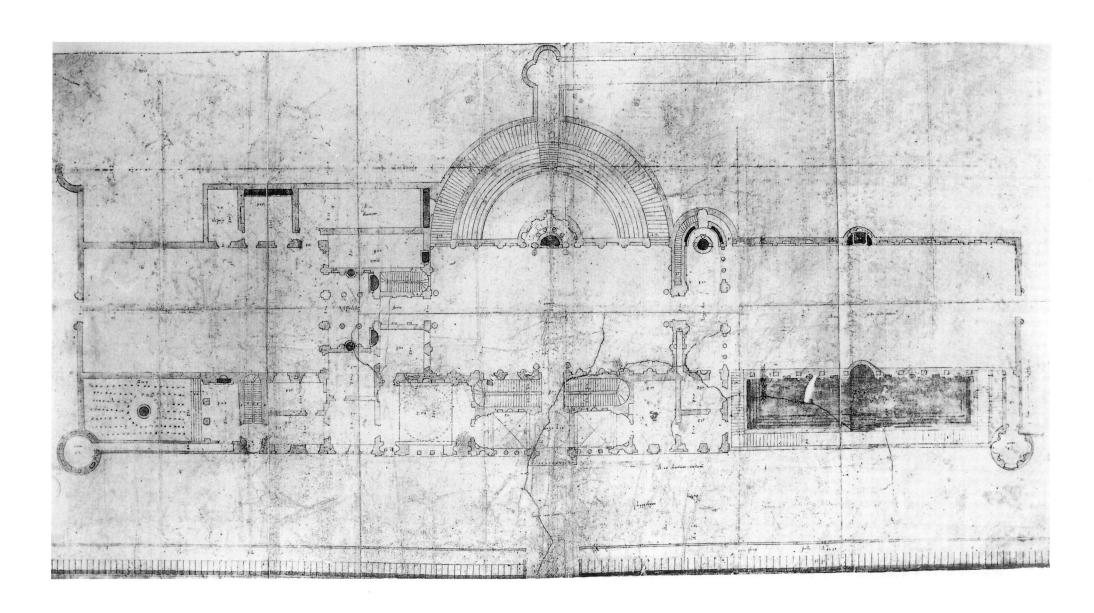

91

Fig. 28 Giovan Francesco Penni: Scene from the Antique

Vienna, Albertina, Graphische Sammlung, no. 231.

The ordonnance of the architectural background is practically the same as that of the North-East and South-West sides of the rectangular court of the U 273 A plan. The analogy is close enough to make it look as though the former had been taken from the latter. Regarding the sunken stairways, these may have answered the requirements of the scene represented but they may just as well have figured, under one form or another, in Raphael's actual project for the court: see paragraph 17, *supra*.

Fig. 29 Raphael: Interior of the Pantheon

Florence, Galleria degli Uffizi, Gabinetto dei Disegni e delle Stampe, no. 164 A v.

Built under Hadrian, the Pantheon was begun in 118 and consecrated by the Emperor between 125 and 128. It owes its preservation to Pope Boniface IV who, in 609, converted it into the church of S. Maria ad Martyres.

This drawing is generally thought to be a Raphael original, made in the years 1506-1507: see John Shearman in *op. cit. note 20 supra*, p. 418. The West half of the interior is represented with three of its four pillars alternating with three columnated exedrae, the last exedra on the right being shown as the entrance arcade which, in reality, faces the apsidal recesses figuring on the left. Apart from the circular shape of the area, which may have led to the conversion of the villa's central court, two of the motifs shown here evidently struck Raphael's fancy. One is that of the pedestaled, columnated and pedimented tabernacles animating the pillars, the other that of the pilaster-enclosed mezzanine windows. The first he adopted for the circular court windows of the villa, as well as for the ground-floor windows of Palazzo Pandolfini, in Florence, and the ambulatory windows of his revised project for St Peter's. The second he adapted to suit the court elevations of Palazzo Branconio da L'Aquila, but allowed it to be, in its original form, misused at the villa.

panteon

Fig. 30 Antoine Desgodetz: Mezzanine windows inside the Pantheon

From *Les edifices antiques de Rome*, by the same, Paris, 1st ed. 1682, 2nd. ed. 1779, Pl. XVIII.

To this day the Desgodetz measured drawings of the Pantheon have not been superseded. A comparison of the plate reproduced here with Fig. 5 *supra*, or Fig. 46 *infra*, shows the completely different size relationships between windows and pilasters such as they exist in the antique model and in the villa: see paragraph 28 *supra*. In the Pantheon, moreover, to make the outer edge of the window surrounds overreach the pilasters, the surround mouldings have been made to protrude more than usual.

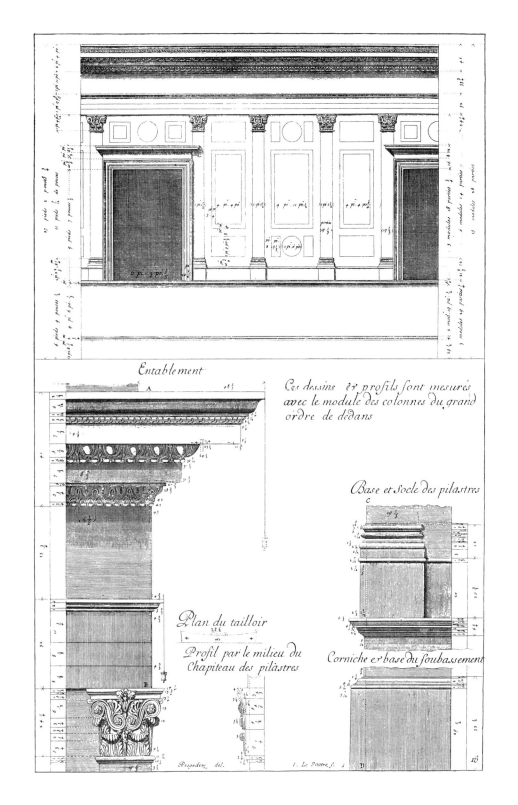

Entablement

Ces dessins & profils sont mesurés
avec le module des colonnes du grand
ordre de dedans

Base et Socle des pilastres

Plan du tailloir

Profil par le milieu du
Chapiteau des pilâstres

Corniche & base du soubassement

Desgodetz del.   I. Le Pautre f.

13

Fig. 31 *Antonio da Sangallo il Giovane: study relating to the outer wall of the ambulatories in Raphael's revised project for St Peter's*

Florence, Galleria degli Uffizi, Gabinetto dei Disegni e delle Stampe, no. 122 A

See C.L. Frommel in *op. cit. note 20 supra*, pp. 241-309, especially pp. 279-288

See Fig. 32 infra.

LEO PAPA

Fig. 32. Studio drawing: early approach to the circular court design
London, R.I.B.A. Drawings Collection, no. XIII-II.

The drawing was first discussed by Howard Burns in *Andrea Palladio 1508-1580*, London 1975, pp. 264-266, then by C.L. Frommel in *op. cit. note 20 supra*, p. 338, and by the same again in the collective work relating to the recent Giulio Romano exhibition in Mantua, published in Milan, 1989, p. 290. To the observations made one might add the following.

The engaged columns of the main order are shown as having a diameter of 4 $^2/_3$ palmi, with inter-axial spacings which amount to about 7 $^1/_2$ times that dimension in the doorway-enclosing bays and 6 times in the bays containing the aedicular windows, to wit 35 palmi in the first case, 28 palmi in the second. Going by the executed work, which was planned to comprise 4 of the larger and 16 of the smaller bays, the perimeter of a court corresponding to the present drawing would reach 588 palmi, with a diameter of 187. Compared to the dimensions of the actual court, which come to 465 palmi for the perimeter and 148 for the diameter, the discrepancy is considerable. It might be interpreted as signifying that the court was originally meant to include no more than 12 of the 16 window bays, thereby bringing the figures down to 476 palmi for the perimeter and 150 for the diameter. But the column diameter of 4 $^2/_3$ palmi, exceeding by $^2/_3$ palmo that adopted in the court, has another effect which is to make the order far too high for the villa. Indeed, corresponding to approximately 13 $^1/_2$ times the diameter of 4 $^2/_3$ palmi, that is 63 palmi, the elevation would have overtopped the upper floor-level by as much as 13 $^2/_3$ palmi, or 3 metres, thereby masking most of the overlying three-sided court enclosure: see Fig. 51 *infra*. Consequently, it very much looks as though this drawing were nothing more than a take-out of Raphael's design for St Peter's, made at a time when the idea of converting the rectangular court of the villa into a circular one was under consideration, the dimensions of the latter being still uncertain. Compared to the Sangallo drawing, reproduced in Fig. 31 *supra*, there is a striking difference: the style of the St Peter's elevation is typically Sangallo's whereas the style of the present drawing is typically Raphael's. It makes one wonder whether the second is not closer to Raphael's original concept for St Peter's, prior to Sangallo's finicking.

Regarding the inscribed dimensions, it is worth noting that the 4 $^1/_2$ palmi height of the pedestal is likely to have been the original dimension, referred to in the commentary to Fig. 54 *infra*, and that the interval of 10 $^1/_4$ palmi, from the pavement up to the window-sill, is in actual fact 11 $^1/_4$ palmi: see Fig. 51 *infra*.

Fig. 33 Antonio da Sangallo il Giovane: Study relating to the execution plan

Florence, Gallerie degli Uffizi, Gabinetto dei Disegni e delle Stampe, no 314 A, detail

Drawn at a scale of $^1/_{350}$ths or thereabouts, the plan is necessarily sketchy: hence the approximate character of certain indications, such as those relating to the entrance court where the depth of the stairway steps and landings is totally inadequate, or to the South-East end of the loggia where the wall ordonnance is grossly misrepresented owing to the problem posed by the spread of the contiguous hall pillar. In the North-West part of the plan, however, there are indications which are quite helpful: such is the inflexion given to the doorway leading from the loggia into the circular court, inflexion which reproduces the curvature of the court, such are the figures concerning the number of steps in the triangular stairway and such is the delineation of the median pilaster discussed in paragraph 10 *supra*.

The nature of the plan corroborates the opinion expressed as to its purpose: that of exposing the problems posed by the introduction of the circulr court and correlative alterations: see paragraphs 20 to 26 *supra*.

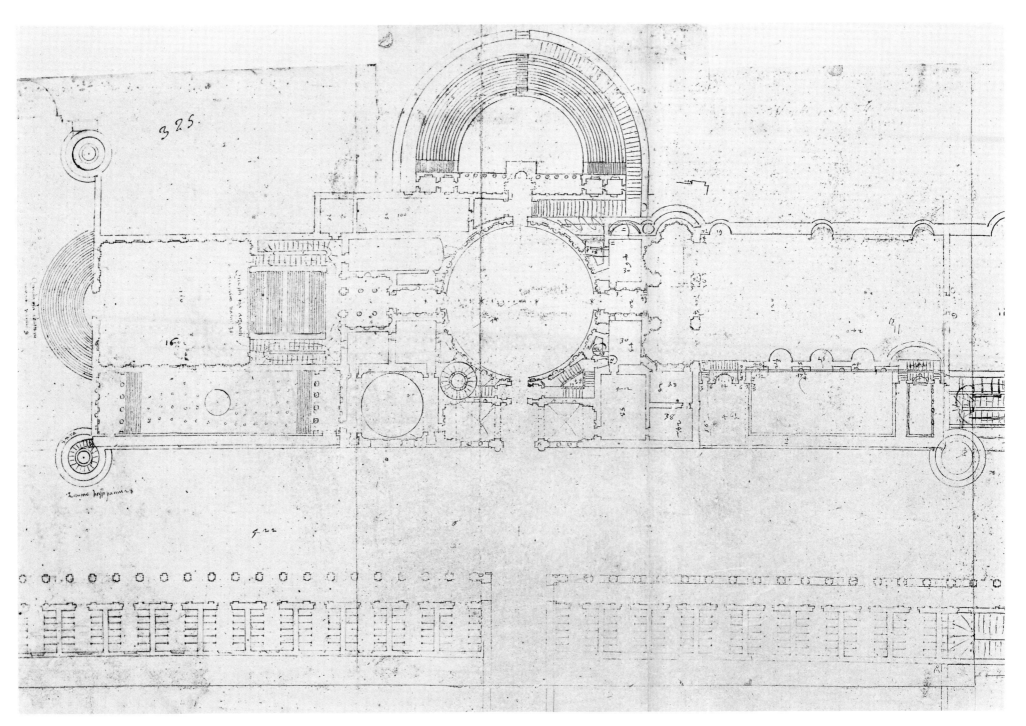

Fig. 34 Antonio de Sangallo il Giovane: Study relating to the entrance court and South-East half of the basement

Florence, Gallerie degli Uffizi, Gabinetto dei Disegni e delle Stampe, no 1518 A, detail

The design of the portal surround, in the far right of the detail reproduced, features a pair of rusticated engaged columns supporting a simple lintel. Running level with the string-course which tops the basement, this lintel was supposed to carry an extruded balustrade similar to that shown in the U 273 A plan. The uniqueness of the design makes it unascribable to anyone but Raphael: it is reconstructed in Fig. 45 *infra*.

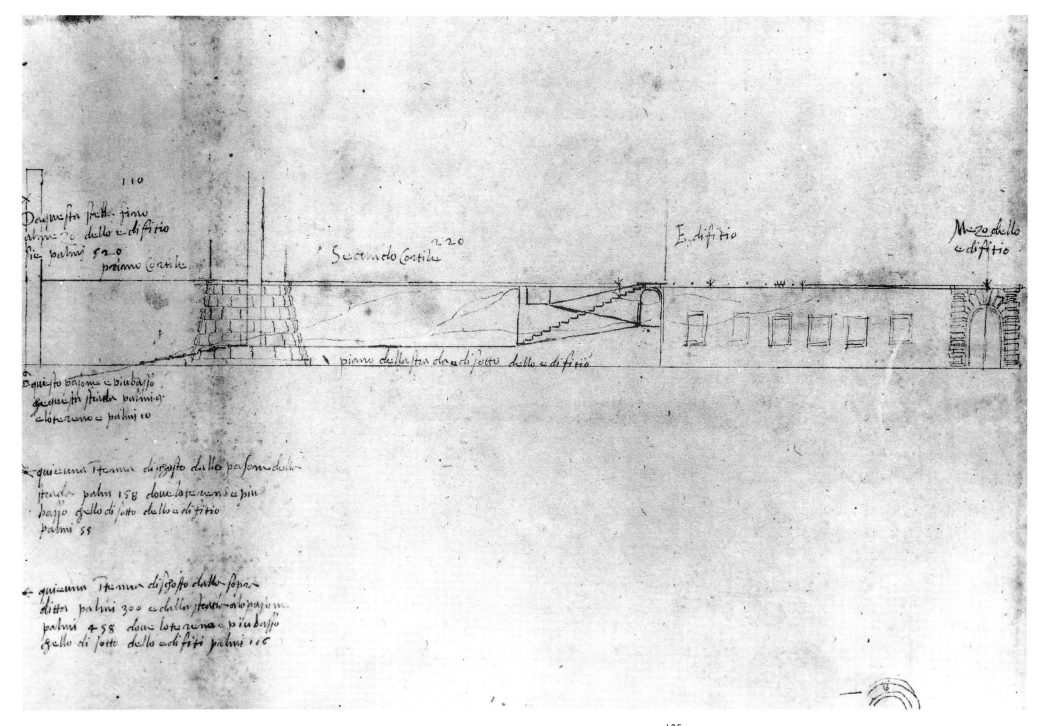

105

Fig. 35 Pietro Ferrerio: Street façade of Palazzo Branconio da L'Aquila, Rome (destroyed)

Palazzi di Roma de' più celebri Architetti, disegnati da Pietro Ferrerio, I, Roma, 1655, fol. 40.

Together with his contribution to the re-building of St Peter's, and his own palace project known only in plan form, this small palace ranks with the villa project as the most characteristic of Raphael's architectural works. He produced the plans for it at the time he was starting to build the villa and it is most likely that in both cases Giulio Romano acted as his personal assistant. Started in the late summer of 1518, construction of the palace was concluded two years later. It has recently been the subject of an excellent survey: see paragraph 28, note 23.

Two items in the façade design are of special interest: the arrangement of the niche-surmounted semi-engaged Doric columns and the stucco decoration of the mezzanine storey: see Figs 63 and 59 B infra.

FACCIATA DEL PALAZZO ET HABBITATIONE DI RAFAELE SANTIO DA VRBINO SV LA VIA DI BORGHONOVO FABRICATO

CON SVO DISEGNO L'ANNO MD·XIII·IN   *Scala Di p.mi Quaranta*
CIRCA·E SEGVITO DA BRAMANTE DA VRBINO

15

Fig. 36 Giulio Romano: *Study relating to the ground level court windows in Palazzo Branconio da L'Aquila, Rome*

Florence, Gallerie degli Uffizi, Gabinetto dei Disegni e delle Stampe, no 1884 A, r.

See paragraphs 28 and 29, plus fig. 30 *supra*.

The drawing belongs in the planning phase of the palace, practically contemporary with that of the villa. The window arrangement, though akin to that in the Pantheon, differs in one essential respect: instead of overreaching the pilasters, the outer edges of the window surround stand well behind and it is only through the artifice of skirting blocks that the clash between the mouldings of the surround and those of the pilaster bases could be avoided. In the adjoining niche design, on the contrary, the conflictual relationship of horizontal and vertical mouldings has been left in full evidence.

Fig. 37 Anonymous draftsman: East façade of court in Palazzo Branconio da L'Aquila, Rome

Florence, Biblioteca Nazionale, Ms II-1-249, fol. 4 r., detail

See paragraphs 28 and 29, plus figs 30 and 51.

The drawing shows how the problems posed by the implementation of the Pantheon type of window were solved by enlarging the engaged columns and substituting a running dado to the pedestals, thereby making the columns rise from the pavement and the window surrounds rest upon the surbase of the dado. Given the circumstances, the arrangement is vastly superior to that shown in Fig. 36 while contributing to turn the whole façade into a most successful composition. It may be worth noting that the setting of window cornices close to an entablature would have been a distinctive feature of the circular court of the villa and is indeed that which gives such a strong character to the first storey of Sansovino's Zecca façade, in Venice.

profilo della faccia del cortile segreto q e una faccia
di fianco la quale ed stucco e sappi ch le prime
finestre cio doue sono e frontoni danno lume alla
scala ch saglie nella prima loggia

Fig. 38 Second storey loggia in the Vatican: Arcade and vault decoration in the fifth compartment

Drawn by C. Savorelli and P. Camporesi, engraved by C. Ottavioni, Rome, 1776-1782.

See paragraph 31.

The side of the compartment reproduced is that of the back wall. Excepting the central motif, the painted part of the decoration is done in trompe-l'oeil as though the windows were part of a screen open to the sky. These windows are devoid of surrounds and surmounted with hanging cornices.

Apparuit Isaac Dominus, et ait: ne descendas in Aegyptum, sed quiesce in terra, quam dixero tibi. Lenes. Cap. XXVI.

Piedi tre ____ di Londra Palmi tre ____ Romani Piedi tre ____ di Parigi

Fig. 39 Th. Hofmann: ground-level plan of the executed work

Reproduced from Th. Hofmann, *op. cit. note 9 supra*, Pl. XLVIII.

As we shall see with Fig. 41, transversally – that is looking North-East - South-West – the reconstruction of Raphael's basic plan poses no problem. It does longitudinally, and in order to clarify matters one must take into account the inter-axial spacing of the superimposed windows in the North-East front of the existing building. To this end the ground-level plan reproduced has been preferred to the superstructure plan, shown in Pl. XLVII of the same work, owing to its greater legibility.

There are six intervals to be considered: 'a' which extends from the transversal axis of the whole scheme to the axis of the cryptoportico window, 'b' from the latter to the axis of the nearest kitchen window, 'c' from the latter to the axis of the other kitchen window, 'd' from the latter to the axis of the nearest service room window, 'e' from the latter to the axis of the other service room window and 'f' from the latter to the outer edge of the concluding pilaster at the North-West end of the superstructure façade.

Among these intervals, quoted in metres, there are three which correspond exactly to dimensions expressed in palmi: 'a', 9.235 metres equal to 41 $\frac{1}{3}$ palmi, 'b', 9.940 metres equal to 44 $\frac{1}{2}$ palmi, 'd', 5.960 metres equal to 26 $\frac{2}{3}$ palmi. There are two which should be identical but are not: 'c' and 'e', the first amounting to 4.5 metres, the second to 4.52 metres, the average dimension being 4.51 metres or approximately 20 $\frac{1}{6}$ palmi. As for interval 'f', this must be taken from Pl. XLVII where it appears as 3.045 metres which corresponds closely to 13 $\frac{2}{3}$ palmi The sum total of the intervals thus comes to 37.200 metres equal to 166 $\frac{1}{2}$ palmi which is half the length of the projected North-East superstructure façade.

The plan reproduced is of further interest in evidencing the fact that the doorway in the apsidal recess was the only means of entering and leaving the kitchen, apart from the service stairway connecting the kitchen dependency with the overlying apartment. It follows that the doorway would have been the normal channel of conveyance for all supplies and all refuse, a circumstance which denotes the utilitarian character of the cryptoportico. At the opposite end of the area a similar doorway was to lead into the baths while the central part of the cryptoportico was evidently to serve as a dismounting place for all riders coming in from Ponte Milvio. Measured drawings of the elevations are reproduced in Fig. 52 *infra*.

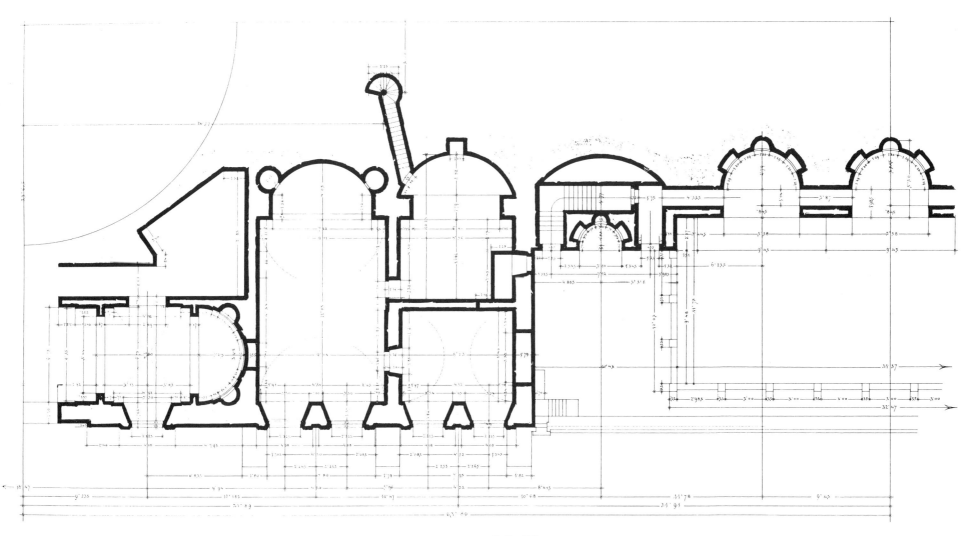

KELLERGESCHOSS.

Aufgenommen von Th. Hofmann, 1890—92.

Fig. 40 GD: *North-East façade of superstructure, comparative plans, A as put into execution, B as reconstructed*

In plan A certain construction irregularities such as variations in the width of the windows have been redressed. The room dimensions and wall thicknesses are those of the actual building: added to the thickness of the North-West façade wall and the protrusion of the North corner pilaster they produce a sum total of 93 ¾ palmi leaving a balance of 73 ¾ palmi for the half-length of the loggia. They put the South-East face of the wall separating the two façade rooms on an alignment which is ⅙ palmo off the middle of the niche within the radiating arcade while the width of the pillars supporting the arcade turns out to be 6⅙ palmi. Since the radius of the arcade is 20⅓ palmi and the height of the arcade casing is 26⅚ palmi, it follows that the interval separating the top of the arcade from the overlying entablature is 6½ palmi, or ⅓ palmo over the width of the pillars.

Plan B proceeds from three reductions, the first in the width of the split pilaster abutting the engaged column of the loggia tribune which is made a round 3 palmi instead of 3⅙, the second in the width of the niche bay of the loggia which is made a round 6 palmi instead of 6½, the third in the thickness of the partition walls which is made a round 4 palmi instead of 4⁵⁄₁₂. The first two reductions, totalling ⅔ palmo, allow an increase of ⅓ palmo each in the width of the radiating arcade pillars thus bringing it up to 6½ palmi and making it equal to the interval at the top of the arcade. The effect of the third is to give the width of the first façade room and the length of the second the same dimensions as those inscribed in the U 314 A plan, to wit 42 and 38 palmi, thereby making the second the same as the first minus the thickness of the partition wall. It is also to place the South-East face of the wall on an alignment passing by the middle of the radiating arcade niche and, finally, it is to turn the half-length of the loggia into a round 73 palmi. For these various reasons there cannot be much doubt that plan B conforms with Raphael's basic project. Further evidence in this respect will be found in figs 41 and 42, the first showing how a generalization of the 4 palmi thickness in the partition walls agrees with the planned room dimensions, the second how the 10 palmi niche bay concurs with the depth of the apsidal recess motif originally meant to occupy both ends of the loggia. It remains to be seen why the longitudinal partition walls of the larger North-East façade room were made thicker and why the width of the niche bay was increased.

To answer the first question one has only to consider the cross-section marked A-B in Fig. 4. In the smaller rooms it is clear that the limited thrust effects of the compound rib-vaulting system would have been absorbed within 4 palmi thick walls. Abutted by the loggia barrel-vault or subjected to the counter-thrusts of the triangular stairwell, room 1 and room 2 vaults, 4 palmi thick longitudinal walls in the larger room would have been equally adequate had the same type of vaulting prevailed. It did not, however, and, with the massive, four-sided, depressed barrel type adopted reinforced walls were evidently required: hence the extra ⁵⁄₁₂ palmo, or 5 oncie put into each.

Continued on p. 120

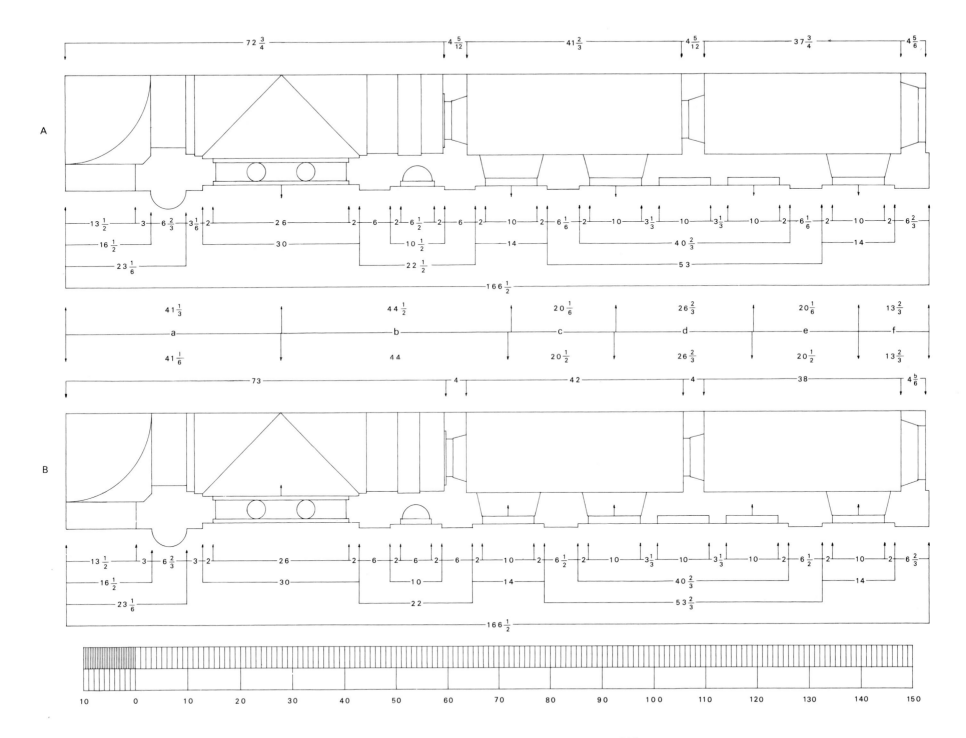

119

The reason for widening the niche bay is far less obvious. On the one hand it naturally increases the visual impact of the motif. On the other, through the correlative reduction in width of the pillars supporting the radiating arcade, it results in making the casing of the arcade thinner at the sides than it is at the top. On both accounts it introduces a perfectly unnecessary perturbation into the elevation. Acting as a simple interconnection between two strong façade elements, those of the loggia and of the radiating arcade, the niche bay hardly needed to be enlarged. There is no more justification in the thinning at the sides of the arcade casing since the $1/2$ palmo excess at the top is totally inadequate for the insertion of a moulding under the entablature. The author therefore suggests that the widening of the niche bay was due to a miscalculation having occurred at the time of setting the basement windows.

Fig. 41 GD: North-West part of superstructure, reconstructed plan of the basic design

See paragraph 20 and figs 39 and 40 *supra*.

The main objective was to integrate the room dimensions of the U 314 A plan into a system of normalized wall thicknesses. The two discrepancies observable are of no consequence. The first is in the room second from the left of the 38 by 28 $1/2$ palmi rooms which, in keeping with Raphael's description, has been given the same dimensions as the first whereas in the U 314 A plan it is marked 38 by 28. The other is in the second room from the left of the 43 by 30 palmi rooms: though clearly of the same size as the first, in the U 314 A plan it is marked 46 by 30.

The wall thicknesses are as follows: 4 $1/2$ palmi for the North-West façade wall, 5 $1/2$ palmi for the three major walls marked A, B, C, and 4 palmi for all partition walls, the 4 $1/2$ and 5 $1/2$ palmi façade walls being brought up to 4 $5/6$ and 5 $5/6$ palmi respectively owing to the extrusion of the panel surrounds mentioned in paragraph 11 *supra*. The thicknesses of 4 $1/2$ and 5 $1/2$ palmi correspond to those of the existing walls whereas the thickness of 4 palmi is an average which, under certain conditions, would have been structurally sound throughout the building. It is to be noted that the South-East face of the wall separating the 58 by 42 palmi room from the pair of 38 by 28 $1/2$ palmi rooms is in line with the vertical axis of the radiating arcade, in the middle of the area taken up by the three rooms.

Conforming with the observations made in paragraph 22 *supra*, in the reconstructed plan the two 43 by 30 palmi rooms have not been shifted, the corresponding apsidal recesses have not been subjected to the correlative reduction in depth and the corridor running slantwise between the contiguous 38 × 28 $1/2$ and 43 × 30 palmi rooms has been suppressed.

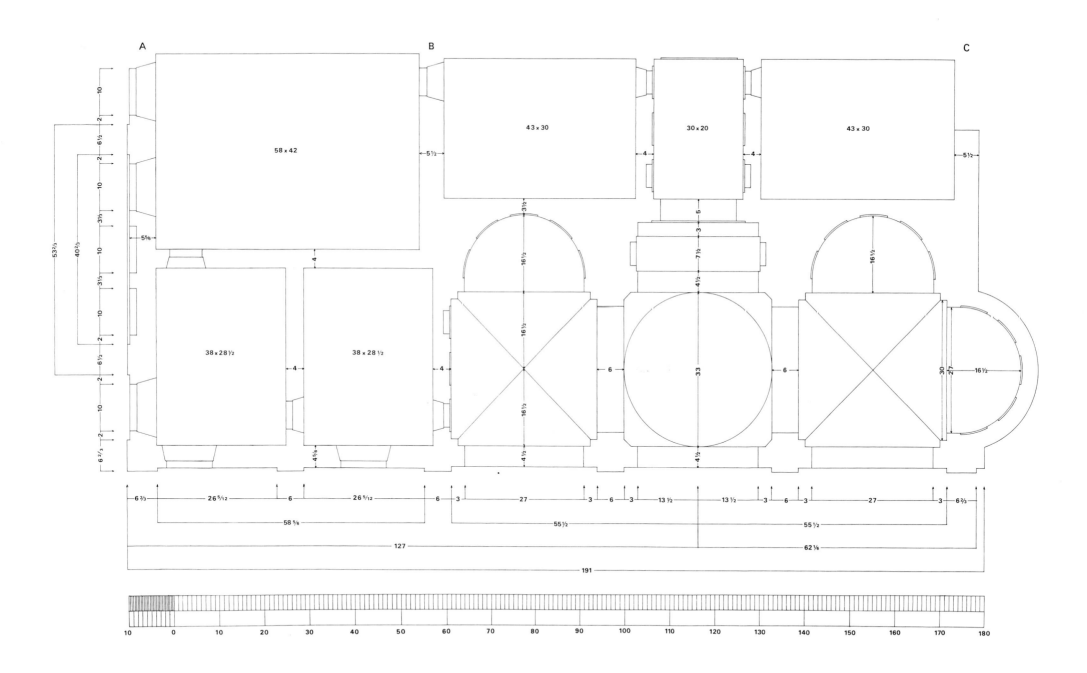

Fig. 42 GD: North-East loggia, reconstructed plan of the basic design

See paragraph 20 *supra*.

We know that the half-length of the superstructure façade is 166 1/2 palmi. By subtracting the length of the part reproduced in Fig. 41, which comes to 86 1/3 palmi, after having added to it the widths of the window jamb and of the pilaster separating the radiating arcade bay from the niche bay: 86 1/3 plus 2 plus 6 equals 94 1/3 palmi; so one obtains a residual figure of 166 1/2 minus 94 1/3 making 72 1/6 palmi to include the half-width of the central bay and the widths of the engaged column bordering it, of the half-pilaster abutting the latter, of the side bay of the loggia, of the pilaster separating the latter from the niche bay and, lastly, of the niche bay. The half-width of the central bay is naturally the same as that of the arcade bays in the North-West façade, or 16 1/2 palmi, whereas the width of the side bay corresponding to the span of the cross-vault, as shown in the U 314 A plan, is 30 palmi. The width of the half-pilaster can only be 3 palmi and that of the pilaster 6, thus bringing the total up to 16 1/2 plus 30 plus 3 plus 6 equals 55 1/2 palmi, and leaving 72 1/6 minus 55 1/2 palmi, or 16 2/3 palmi for the thickness of the engaged column and the width of the niche bay. It seems appropriate that the thickness of the column should be the same as the width of the North angle pilaster, thereby making it 6 2/3 palmi and leaving 10 palmi for the width of the niche bay. Admittedly, such a thickness for a column which is only a trifle over 8 times as high might be deemed excessive but it is not if one considers the arrangement of which the column is a part: see fig. 59 B *infra*.

In the commentary to Fig. 40 we saw that the width of 10 palmi for the niche bay concurs with the depth of the apsidal recesses originally meant to form the ends of the loggia. The motif is outlined here, the semicircular line marking the springing of the hemispherical vault as well as the setting of the pilasters which were to subdivide the wall area. It is to be noted that the actual wall would therefore have stood 1/3 palmo behind the line in the same way as it stands 1/3 palmo behind the casing of the central niche in the orthogonal arrangement. It is also to be noted that the extra 1/3 palmo should be included in the sum of the loggia subdivisions to arrive at the half-length of 73 palmi.

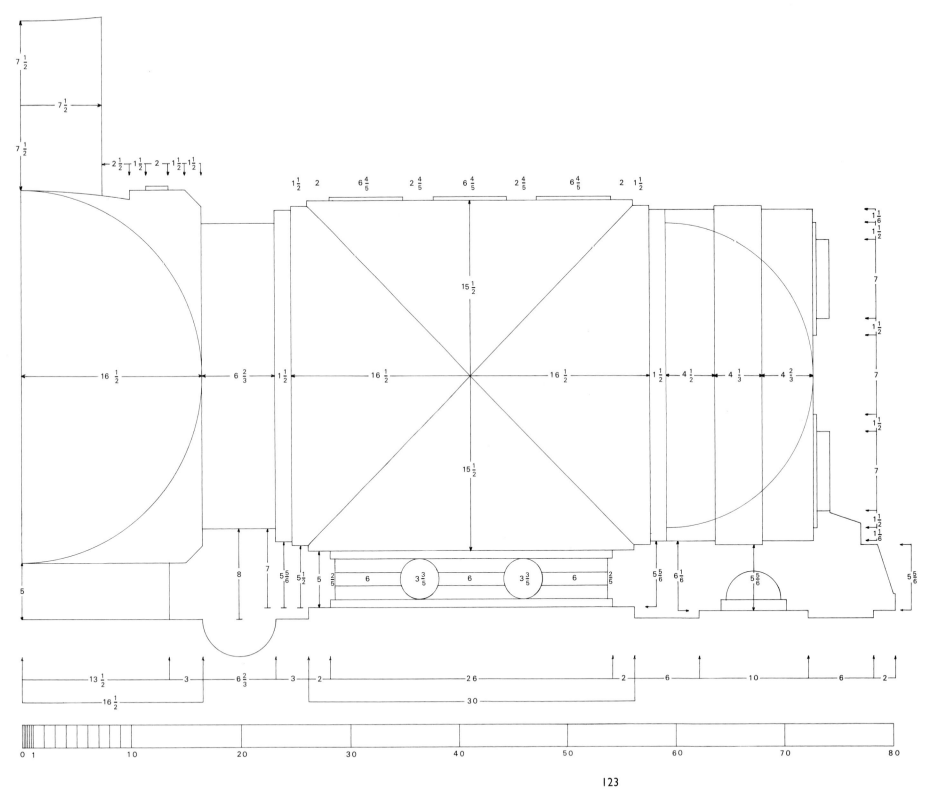

123

Fig. 43 GD: *North-West half of complex, reconstructed plan of the basic design*

The plan proceeds from the conclusions arrived at in the commentaries to Figs 39 to 42 *supra* and, for the terrace-garden and the fishpond, to the indications provided by the U 314 A plan and the executed work. Not including the towers, the total length of the basement would have amounted to 168 plus 235 plus 9 making 412 palmi which, multiplied by 2 makes 824 palmi. At the superstructure level, the total length of the complex would have been 4 palmi less, owing to a 2 palmi recession of the terminal precinct walls from those of the underlying basement, thus bringing it down to 820 palmi, or 82 canne. Conforming with the dimension of 522 palmi, inscribed in the U 314 A plan as that of the half-length of the platform supporting the complex, the total length of the reconstructed platform comes to 1044 palmi.

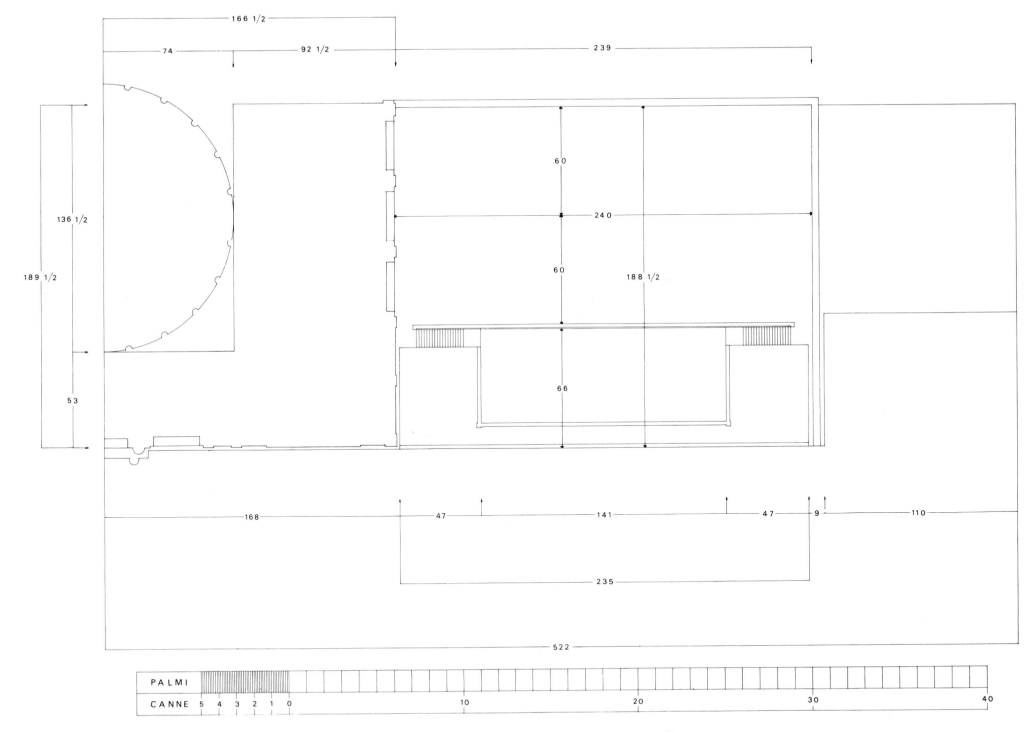

Fig. 44 GD : *A reconstruction of the U 3I4 A plan*

The entrance court is 110 by 240 palmi. In the original the length of the lower court is marked 160 palmi, leaving only 80 palmi for that of the upper court which is totally inadequate. To achieve practicability the reconstructed stairway has been made 90 palmi long and the top landing 20 palmi wide, thereby reducing the length of the lower court to 130 palmi. At the same time the level of the latter has been raised by 1 palmo which gives its ordonnance a height of 33 palmi corresponding to 44 risers of $3/4$ palmo, or 40 steps set in four flights of 10 with three intermediary landings, the treads being 1$1/2$ palmi and the landings 10 palmi wide. With this arrangement, the gradient of the side ramps comes to 15.71%.

The reconstructed walled-in garden is 52$1/2$ by 194 palmi, its width being 2$1/2$ palmi less than that specified by Raphael. But the reduction is inevitable if, in spite of the inadequacy commented upon in paragraph 33 *supra*, one wishes to respect Raphael's intention of protecting the garden by means of a wall backed by a corridor leading from the superstructure to the East tower. The wall is 4$1/3$ palmi thick, the corridor is 8 palmi wide and its garden-side wall is 2$1/2$ palmi. The depth of the garden porticoes is 20 palmi, their columns have a diameter of 3 palmi with an intercolumniation of 7$1/2$ palmi, or 2$1/2$ diameters.

The prime function of the towers was evidently to mark the corners of the complex. Their diameter is 40 palmi externally, 30 palmi internally, or 8.94 and 6.70 m. respectively. We know that Raphael thought of using the East tower as a dieta, the North tower as a chapel. But he gives the structures a diameter of 60 palmi, or 13.40 m., implying an internal one of 60 palmi, or 10.72 m., these dimensions clearly suiting his purpose : see the reconstruction of Raphael's early project in Fig. 53 *infra*. The reduction made suggests that his ideas were not followed up, the difficulty of connecting the existing terrace-garden with an eventual North tower adding weight to the assumption. As an alternative, Room 5 would have made a suitable chapel, room 6 a sacristy.

We have seen that the proper length of the North-East loggia is twice 73 palmi, or 146 palmi. The great hall is as long as the area occupied by the North-East apartment is wide, to wit 42 plus 4 plus 38 making 84 palmi, and the domical vault of the hall has been given a diameter of 50 palmi. Structurally, the hollowing of the massive pillars supporting the vault would have called for the insertion of a relieving and buttressing arcade within the uper part of each pillar, added to which the North-East-South-West spread of the pillars would necessarily have been greater than that shown by Sangallo, thereby precluding his positioning of the loggia doorway. In fact this doorway could only have been placed in line with its faked counterpart, at the opposite end of the loggia, an alternating disposition in keeping with Raphael's predilection for paired doorways, one true, the other false.

At the South-West side of the hall, rooms 11 and 12 are respectively 39 by 43 palmi and 29 by 39. The wall in between is the only transversal partition wall to have been given a thickness in excess of 4 palmi: conforming with that of the arcade standing between the entrance portico and the lobby, it is 5 palmi. As pointed out in

25 *supra*, the stairway adjoining the common room, or room 10, would have been the only means of access to the attic storey. In the reconstruction the stairway is designed to comprise four flights of 6 palmi wide steps with $1^1/_2$ palmi treads and $^2/_3$ palmo risers, the lower flight incorporating 17 steps and each one of the other three 18.

The circular court is the essential part of the villa. A plan of the half-completed structure may be seen in Fig. 2, an elevation in Fig. 4, a general view in Fig. 7, details of the ordonnance in Fig. 25 and a tentative reconstruction of the whole design in Fig. 51. The diameter of the circumference passing through the centre of the large engaged columns is 148 palmi, the wall being slightly set back to prevent the curvature from infringing upon the basic half-diameter of the shafts. We shall see presently that this diameter is 4 palmi, that of the aedicular columns $2^1/_5$. Expressed in $^1/_{90}$ths of the rectangular angle, the angle formed by the radii intersecting the circumference at the centre of two consecutive columns amounts to 17 degrees in the case of the windowed bay, 22 degrees in that of the doorway bays and 10 in that of the aedicular windows. Had the court been completed, its relatively considerable extent would certainly have called for the construction of a monumental fountain in its centre : it is a matter of importance for an appreciation of the design.

Like that of the entrance court, though to a lesser degree, the U 3I4 A theatre design is an unaccomplished one, unsympathetically rendered by Sangallo. To meet the requirements of a hillside precinct destined to accommodate performing artists and their audience it fails in two respects. In the first place, the sole means of access to the various parts of the theatre being via the top of the auditorium, at the conclusion of a long ramp issuing from the circular court, the performers, the staff and the audience would have been subjected to an inordinately long perambulation on entering and leaving the theatre. In the second place, the auditorium benches drawn by Sangallo are inadequately dimensioned to answer the purpose of seating each a double row of audience members, one sitting upon the bench, the other sitting upon the next with feet resting behind the first. The first impropriety could have been remedied by opening a passage between the stage and the auditorium, thereby providing a direct access to the orchestra and the other low-lying parts of the theatre. Such a type of entry was common in the theatres of antiquity, whether Greek or Roman, and there is very little likelihood of Raphael having been unaware of the fact. In the present instance, the passage could have been made 10 palmi wide, or 2.234 metres, and the auditorium reduced accordingly or, better still, set deeper in the hillside. The second impropriety has been redressed, in the reconstructed plan, by bringing down the number of benches from 11 to 7, thus giving each one a height and depth of 2 and $4^1/_2$ palmi respectively, or 0.447 and 1.005 m. Likewise, the continuous ramp has been replaced by a stairway comprising nine flights of 10 steps each, with $^2/_3$ palmo risers, the total difference in levels reaching 66 palmi. Thanks to the eight intermediary landings, 10 palmi wide, such a stairway would have been easier to ascend than a ramp, the gradient of which would have reached 26.40%. Conversely, the ramp would have made the top of the auditorium accessible to horse and mule-mounted personages but one fails to see where the mounts and their attendants might have been stationed during performances, unless it were down the South-East counterpart of the ramp which re-descends to reach the level of the stage.

The tribune forming the central part of the stage clearly comes from Fra Giocondo's somewhat fancifull reconstruction of the Roman theatre. The centre of curvature of the auditorium is at the edge of the tribune and it is by drawing a line across from here to its points of intersection with the edge of the auditorium platform that one obtains the lower side of the Vitruvian equilateral triangle, the other sides joining up at the top of the circumference formed by the outer edge of the auditorium enclosure. In the reconstructed plan, the stage is at the same level as the platform of the auditorium, 14 palmi below the top of the theatre and 52 palmi above the circular court, the last interval giving ample space to accommodate, at court level, a grotto such as that figuring under the stage in the U 314 A plan. Not including the thickness of the wall enclosing the peripheral ramp, the diameter of the theatre comes to 216 palmi and that of the orchestra to 50% less, or 108 palmi. The auditorium might have accommodated 360 people.

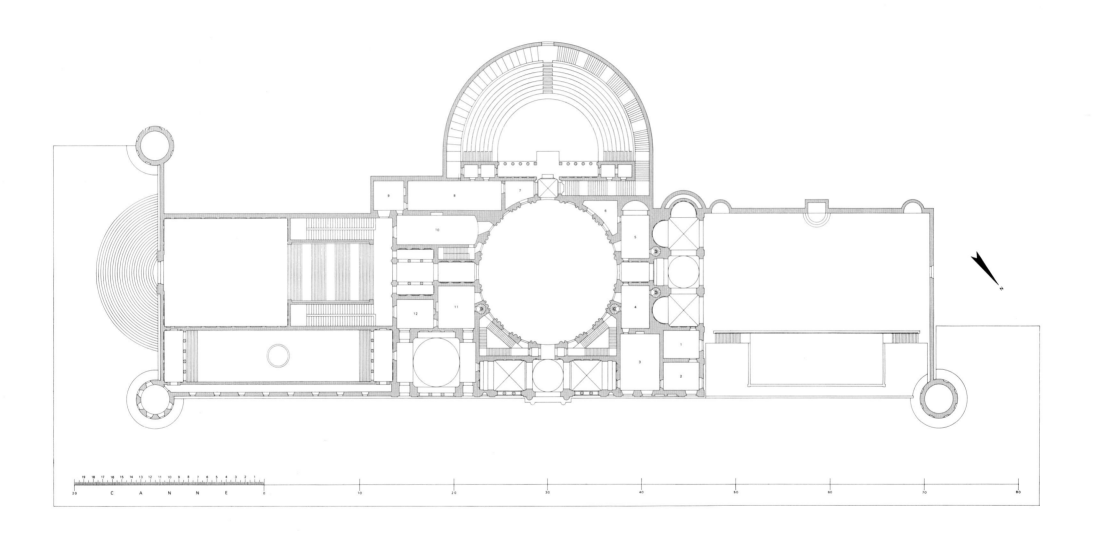

Fig. 45 GD: Reconstruction of basement portal

See Fig. 34 supra: the reconstruction is a simple adaptation of the Sangallo sketch to the dimensions of the building.

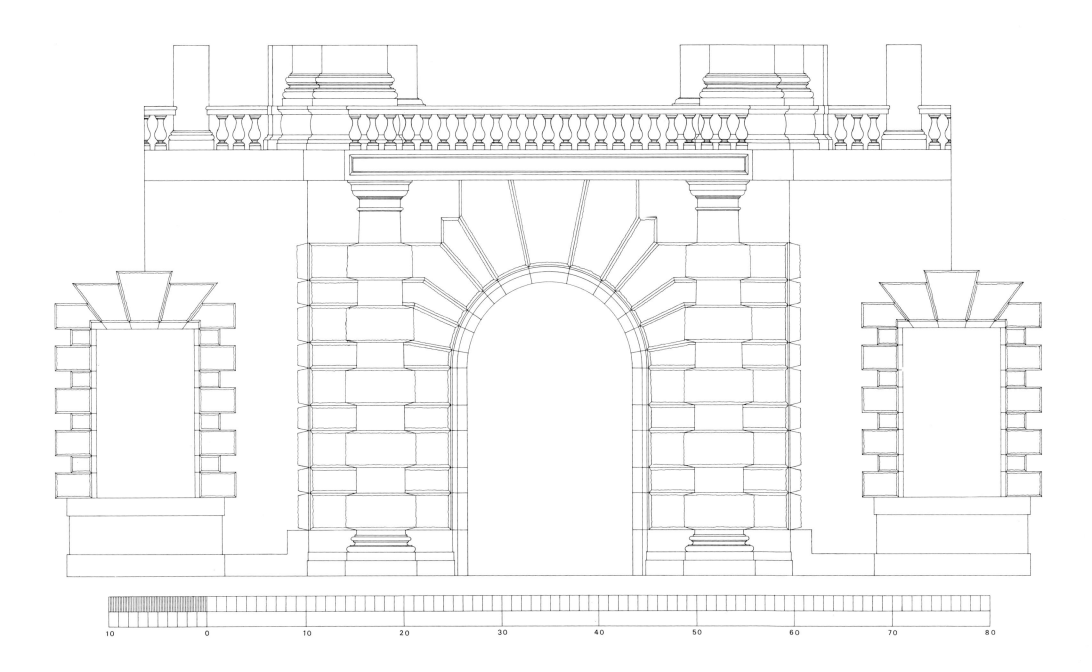

Fig. 46 GD: Superstructure elevations, windowed bay at North-East end of the North-West façade

See commentaries to figs. 13, 23, 40 and 41 *supra*, and 47 *infra*.

We have seen that the North corner pilaster is thicker than the others: to appreciate the order one should therefore consider the pilaster standing at the right of the first. Not counting the pedestal, the height of the pilaster, including the capital and the base, is 53 $^2/_3$ palmi which, in terms of the module, comes to 12 modules and $^1/_3$rd. Including the entablature, the height of the order comes to 61 $^1/_6$ palmi, equalling 22 modules and $^7/_{18}$ths, and including the pedestal it comes to 71 $^1/_2$ palmi, equalling 23 modules and $^5/_6$ths. The wall area comprised between the pedestal and the entablature is vertically divided into three by two string-courses of which the lower, continuing in a simplified form the imposts of the portico arcades, is 2$^5/_6$ palmi, equalling $^{17}/_{18}$ths of the module height, while the upper, delimiting a frieze-like area under the entablature, is 2 palmi, which equals $^2/_3$rds of the module, the combined heights of both coming to 4$^5/_6$ palmi, equalling 1 module and $^{11}/_{18}$ths.

The ridge of the lower string-course subdivides the wall area, from the pedestal to the entablature, into two main parts each of which is 26 $^5/_6$ palmi, equalling 8 modules and $^{17}/_{18}$ths high. The aperture of the window is 10 by 16 $^2/_3$ palmi, or 3 modules and $^1/_3$rd by 5 modules and $^5/_9$ths, the jambs and lintel being 2 palmi or $^2/_3$rds of a module thick. The height of the cornice and accompanying string course is 1 $^1/_2$ palmi – not 1 $^1/_3$ as shown by Hofmann – or $^1/_2$ a module. The blank area at the right of the window is a design inadequacy ascribable to Giulio Romano. The height of the frieze under the entablature is 8 palmi equalling 2 modules and $^2/_3$rds. The frieze was evidently meant to be decorated, as were the panels: it is to be remembered that the frieze and the field of the panels are on the same upright.

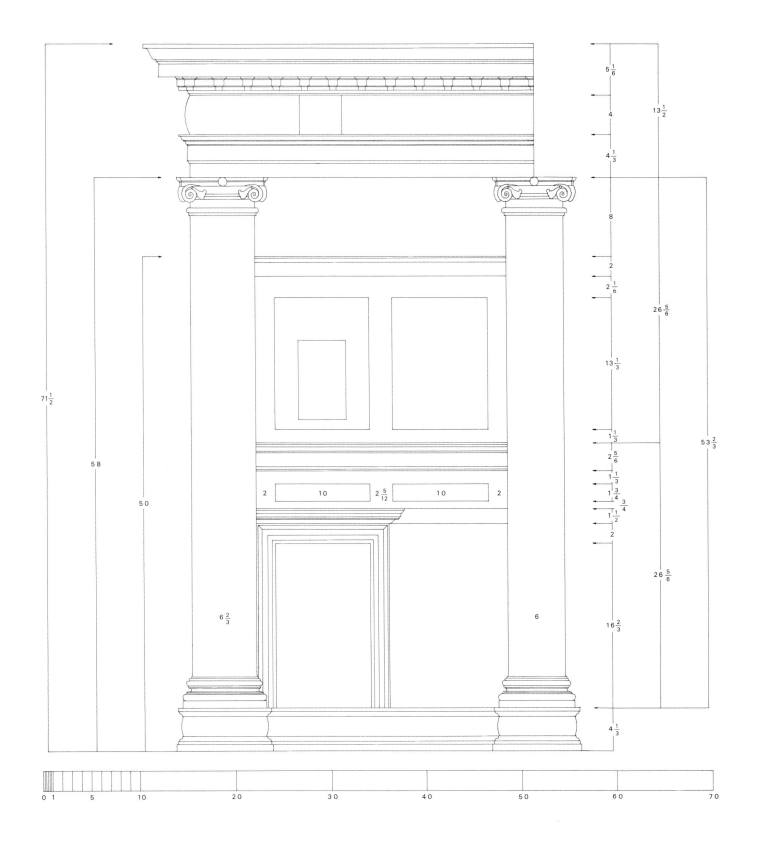

$71\frac{1}{2}$

58

50

$6\frac{2}{3}$

2 10 $2\frac{5}{12}$ 10 2

6

$5\frac{1}{6}$

4

$13\frac{1}{2}$

$4\frac{1}{3}$

8

2

$2\frac{1}{6}$

$26\frac{5}{6}$

$13\frac{1}{3}$

$1\frac{1}{3}$

$2\frac{5}{6}$

$1\frac{1}{3}$

$1\frac{3}{4}$

$\frac{3}{4}$

$1\frac{1}{2}$

2

$53\frac{2}{3}$

$26\frac{5}{6}$

$16\frac{2}{3}$

$4\frac{1}{3}$

0 1   5   10   20   30   40   50   60   70

Fig. 47 GD: Superstructure elevations, arcaded bay of the North-West portico

See Fig. 46 *supra.*

The arcaded bay is the basic element in the North-East and North-West façades of the superstructure. Inter-axially, the spacing of the pilasters is 39 palmi equalling 13 modules, the intercolumniation is 33 palmi or 11 modules, the width of the arcade opening is 27 palmi or 9 modules and the width of the jambs is 3 palmi equalling 1 module.

The centre of curvature of the arch is set 1 $\frac{1}{3}$ palmi ($\frac{4}{9}$ths of the module) above the ridge-line of the impost, thus giving the arcade opening a height of 46 palmi, equal to 15 modules and $\frac{1}{3}$rd. Other simple interrelations between the arcaded bay and the order are as follows: at 13 $\frac{1}{2}$ palmi the radius of the opening is the same as the height of the entablature, at 3 palmi the width of the arcade jambs and of the archivolt is $\frac{1}{9}$th of the width of the opening whereas, at 6 palmi the thickness of the pilasters is $\frac{2}{9}$ths of the same, and at 9 palmi the height of the spandrel area taken from the tip of the archivolt is $\frac{3}{9}$ths.

Affording an extensive area for decorative purposes at spandrel level, the beautifully proportioned bay is characteristic of Raphael's architectural style.

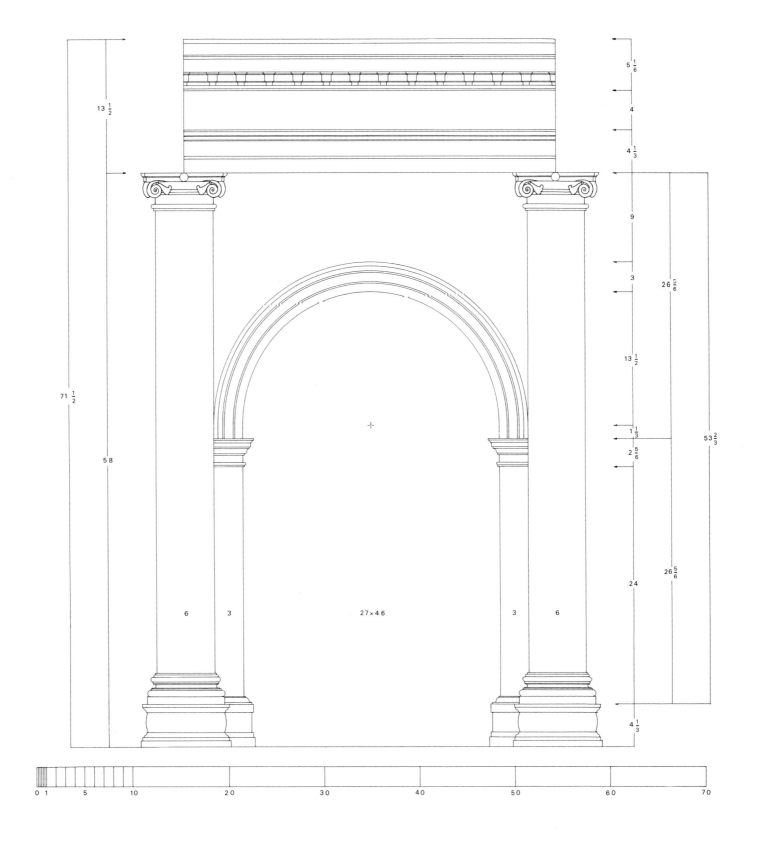

13 $\frac{1}{2}$

71 $\frac{1}{2}$

58

5 $\frac{1}{6}$

4

4 $\frac{1}{3}$

9

3

13 $\frac{1}{2}$

1 $\frac{1}{3}$

2 $\frac{5}{6}$

26 $\frac{5}{6}$

26 $\frac{5}{6}$

53 $\frac{2}{3}$

24

4 $\frac{1}{3}$

6   3

27 x 4 6

3   6

0 1   5   10   20   30   40   50   60   70

Fig. 48 GD : North-West half of superstructure, a reconstruction of the projected North-East and North-West elevations

Including the central bay of the NE loggia, the reconstruction naturally conforms with the conclusions reached in the commentaries to Figs 40 to 42, and the views expressed in paragraph 27 *supra*. Taken from the example reproduced in Fig. 38, the decorative scheme applied to the radiating arcade has the effect of turning the entire wall area of which it forms a part, within the two enclosing pilasters, into one architectural unit. Since the arcade stands on the same upright as the pilasters, once stuccoed it would have merged with the lower fascia in the entablature. To achieve a differentiation, the one and only means would have been through a chromatic contrast. Moreover, it is only by means of such a contrast that the low-relief ornamentation of the façades could have been made visible from afar. It follows that Raphael's intention was certainly to limit the application of the usual Travertine-like stucco coating to the main horizontal and vertical parts of the ordonnance and to use a coloured intonaco for the rest: see Fig. 59 B *infra*.

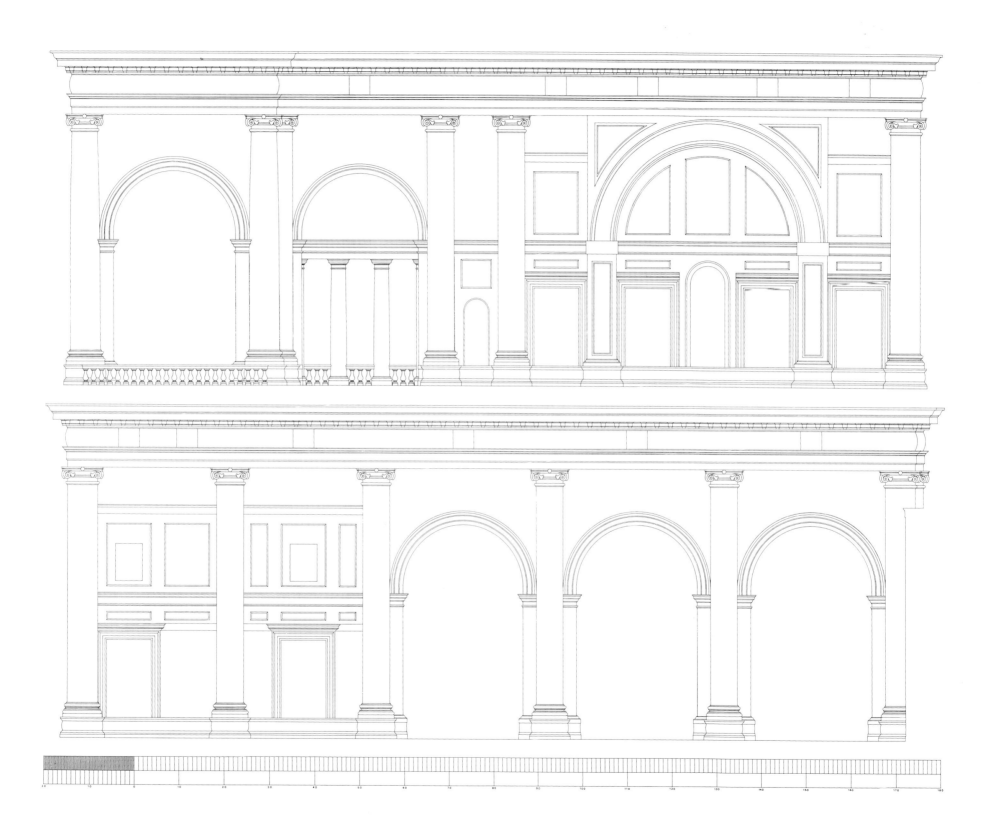

Fig. 49 GD : *Wall design at the North-East end of the North-West portico and reconstructed wall design at the North-West end of the North-East loggia*

The wall of the portico is on the left, that of the loggia on the right. The first is to be considered in relation with the view and the plan reproduced in Figs 14 and 41 *supra*, the second in relation with those reproduced in figs 7 and 42.

In the portico, the three-tier arrangement prevails throughout, whether the walls are plane or curved. Since the latter have a larger surface area, however, they incorporate five instead of three bays. The pilasters are 3 palmi wide in the plane areas and, in the curved areas, the angle at which their sides are set make them practically the same. The width of the double-edged niches is 4 $1/6$ palmi externally, 3 $2/3$ palmi internally. There again, the dimensions of those which are radially set are very much the same but the width of their jambs is smaller. The protrusion of the pilasters is $1/3$ palmo while the depth of the indentation, at the edges of the niches, is $2/3$.

In Fig. 41, the apsidal recesses have been given back their original configuration. The diameter of the semi-circumference skirting the intermediary pilasters is in line with the inner side of the pilasters bordering the apsidal recess, 3 palmi within the recess. The radius is 13 $1/2$ palmi, the perimeter of the half-circumference is about 42 $1/5$ palmi. Expressed in $1/90$ths of the rectangular angle, and going from left to right, the angles of the radii determining the setting of the pilaters are as follows : 26 and 38 $1/2$ degrees, 64 $1/2$ and 77, 103 and 115 $1/2$, 141 $1/2$ and 154, whereas those of the radii forming the axes of the niches are : 13 degrees, 51 $1/2$, 90, 128 $1/2$ and 167.

The reconstruction of the loggia wall is based on the view reproduced in Fig. 7. The lower tier underlying the niche is the same as in the portico. Of the big doorways, the aperture of which is 7 palmi, or 1.56 m., crosswise, the one on the left is a sham, the one on the right leads into the main room of the North-West apartment. The string-course issuing from the niche entablature runs even with the cornices of the façade windows: see Fig. 46 *supra*. It was certainly meant to be carried across the back walls of the loggia where it would have been supported by the pilasters 2 $4/5$ palmi wide, rising from the pavement, most probably with a pedimented niche in the central bay of each: see paragraph 9 *supra*. To appreciate the effect of the end wall design one should imagine it with a statue in the niche, a bas-relief in the lower tier panel and a running decoration in the frieze.

Fig. 50 GD: North-West portico, isometric perspective of the returned apsidal recesses

The purpose of the perspective is to illustrate the effect discussed in the commentary to Fig. 14 *supra*. The two recesses are shown as being identical, which is certainly as they were intended, whereas that on the right was in fact internally fitted with an extra pilaster on either side of its aperture. This is a consequence of the tampering with the court-side recesses described in paragraph 22 *supra*, the extra pilasters being required to compensate, in this particular case, for the ensuing loss of depth.

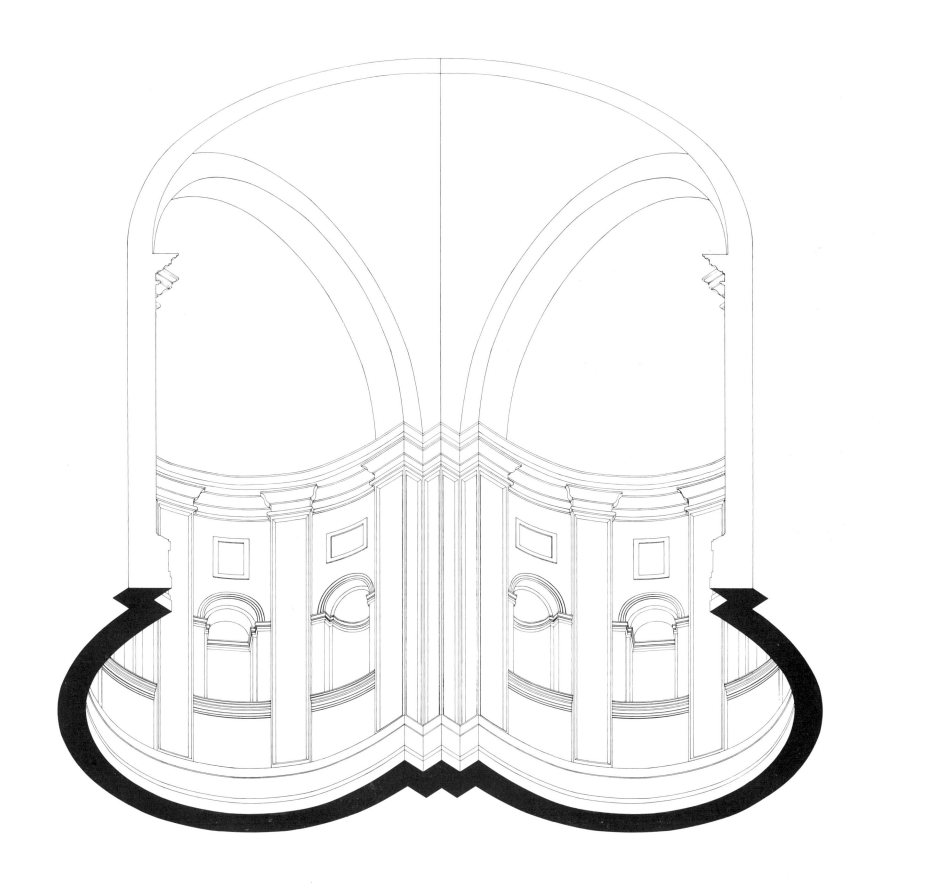

Fig. 51 GD : Reconstructed ordonnance of the circular court

See Figs 2, 4, 7, 25, 32 and 44 *supra.*

The developed elevation shows one of the four doorway bays and two of the sixteen window bays. Owing to the radial setting of the columns, defined in the commentary to Fig. 44, the inscribed inter-axial dimensions are approximate: they total 465 $^1/_5$ palmi against a true perimeter which is just under 465.

Up to the top of the entablature surmounting the aedicular columns, and excepting the doorway bays, the elevation reproduced is exactly as executed. The reconstructed parts of the design are the doorway surround, the top of the main columns, with their capitals, the main entablature and its pedestal-like parapet. The void of the doorway naturally correponds to the dimensions of the various lobbies : it is 15 palmi crosswise and, as shown in Fig. 65 *infra*, 28 $^2/_3$ palmi high. The height of the main columns corresponds to 9 times their diameter, amounting to 36 palmi, that of the entablature to 2 $^1/_4$ times the diameter, amounting to 9 palmi, such ratios applied to the Ionic order tending to become institutionalized in Raphael's day. It follows that the height of the ordonnance, minus that of the parapet, comes to 49 $^1/_3$ palmi, or $^2/_3$ palmi below the attic storey level.

In keeping with the drawing reproduced in Fig. 32 *supra*, a decorative recess has been inserted into the wall area surmounting the entablature of the aedicular windows. There are three good reasons for retaining this item: it creates a striking relationship with the aperture of the window, it ties the aedicular structure to the rest of the ordonnance and it concurs with the indications concerning ornementation we shall come to presently. In the reconstruction, the item is 4 $^1/_3$ palmi square.

At 24 $^3/_4$ palmi, the height of the aedicular order amounts to 11 $^1/_4$ times the column diameter of 2 $^1/_5$ palmi, which ratio corresponds to the sum total of the ratios referred to in connection with the reconstruction of the main order. But, here, the repartition between column and entablature is slightly different, their respective heights of 20 $^7/_{20}$ palmi and 4 $^2/_5$ amounting to 9 $^1/_4$ times the diameter for the first and to twice the diameter for the second. The entablature is devoid of a cymatium, the corona being topped with a simple cavetto-supported fillet, and it is therefore natural that it should be slimmer. The reason for the apparent transfer to the height of the column of the $^1/_4$ diameter, or $^{11}/_{20}$ palmo, missing in that of the entablature is far less clear. In relation with the Ionic capitals of the executed work, it might be accounted for by a wish to underline the capital with a neck decoration as shown in the reconstruction. But the capitals are re-used, ill-designed, late antique pieces which are most unlikely to have been Raphael's choice. It is possible, therefore, that the lengthening of the column was due to his intention of adopting a capital of composite design.

A significant feature in the aedicular entablature is that it is set back $^1/_{20}$ palmo, or 0.011 m., from its normal upright passing by the top of the column. The implication is that the frieze was meant to be decorated, a

(continued on p. 144)

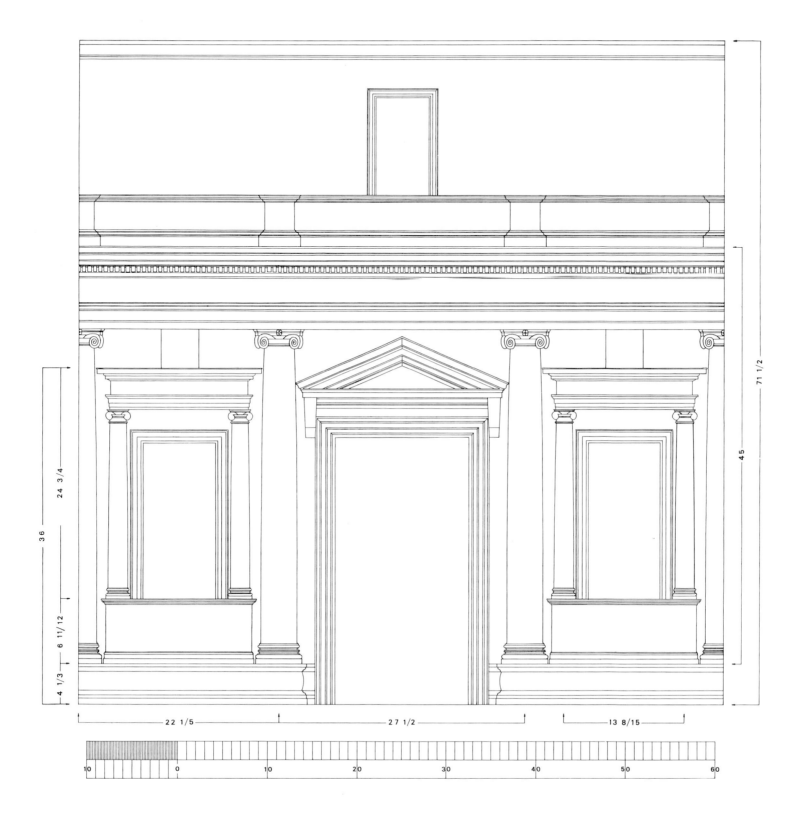

71 1/2

45

36

24 3/4

6 11/12

4 1/3

22 1/5

27 1/2

13 8/15

10   0   10   20   30   40   50   60

circumstance which makes it highly probable that another area, that over lying the window surround, was meant to be too. Hence the reference earlier made to ornamentation.

The present restitution supersedes that presented in the first edition of the memoir in which the height of the aedicular pedestal was put at 5 $^{1}/_{2}$ palmi instead of being given its true dimension of 6 $^{11}/_{12}$. The occurrence is all the more regrettable since it deprived the ordonnance of one of its princial merits : the kinetic effect produced by the difference in levels at which the doorway and window entablatures come to rest. It is worth noting that the effect is also absent from the design elaborated by Sangallo for St Peter's, in the U 122 A drawing reproduced in Fig. 31 *supra*. Moreover, it is a fact that an ordonnance such as this is far better suited to the concavity of the court than it was to the external convexity of the St Peter's ambulatories.

*Illustrations
Section 5:*

A reconstruction of Raphael's early design

Fig. 52 Pietro Garau: Elevations of the cryptoportico

See Fig. 39. These measured drawings were made, in 1976, to complement the Hofmann plan. The cryptoportico is impossible to photograph owing to the presence of a fuel tank occupying practically the whole space.

The reason for including the cryptoportico in the section relating to Raphael's early design is that the interval between the crossing of the vaults and the tip of the apsidal recess is 7.075 metres or 31 $\frac{2}{3}$ palmi and that, added to a $\frac{1}{3}$ palmi setting back of the wall in relation with the ring of pilasters supporting the vault, it comes to exactly the same dimension as that of the corresponding interval in the loggia of the U 273 A plan.

Construction irregularities are more important than at the superstructure level. Varying slightly with the measurements taken, the following seem to have been the planned dimensions: the area covered by the ribs of the cross-vault should be 29 palmi lengthwise, 22 palmi crosswise, and the radius of the apsidal recess being half the expanse of the longitudinal vault should be 14 $\frac{1}{2}$. The wall protrusions, at the springing of the ribs, are 3 palmi wide while the thickness of the arcade separating the cross-vaulted unit from the apsidal recess is also 3 palmi. Consequently the interval between the vault crossing and the tip of the apsidal recess should be 11 plus 3 plus 3 plus 14 $\frac{1}{2}$ equal to 31 $\frac{1}{2}$ palmi against 31 $\frac{2}{3}$ in actual fact.

The way the vaults are sprung is an exercise in stilting. The arcade separating the cross-vaulted unit from the apsidal recess, the hemispheric vault of the latter and the blind arcade in the back wall of the cryptoportico are all set 1 palmo above the running impost, whereas the cross-vaults are set another 1 palmo higher. The effect of the arrangement is best seen in the elevation of the back wall and in that containing the doorway, in the apsidal recess. Owing to the different spans of the cross-vaults these naturally give rise to a supplementary, web-like, domical vault at their intersection.

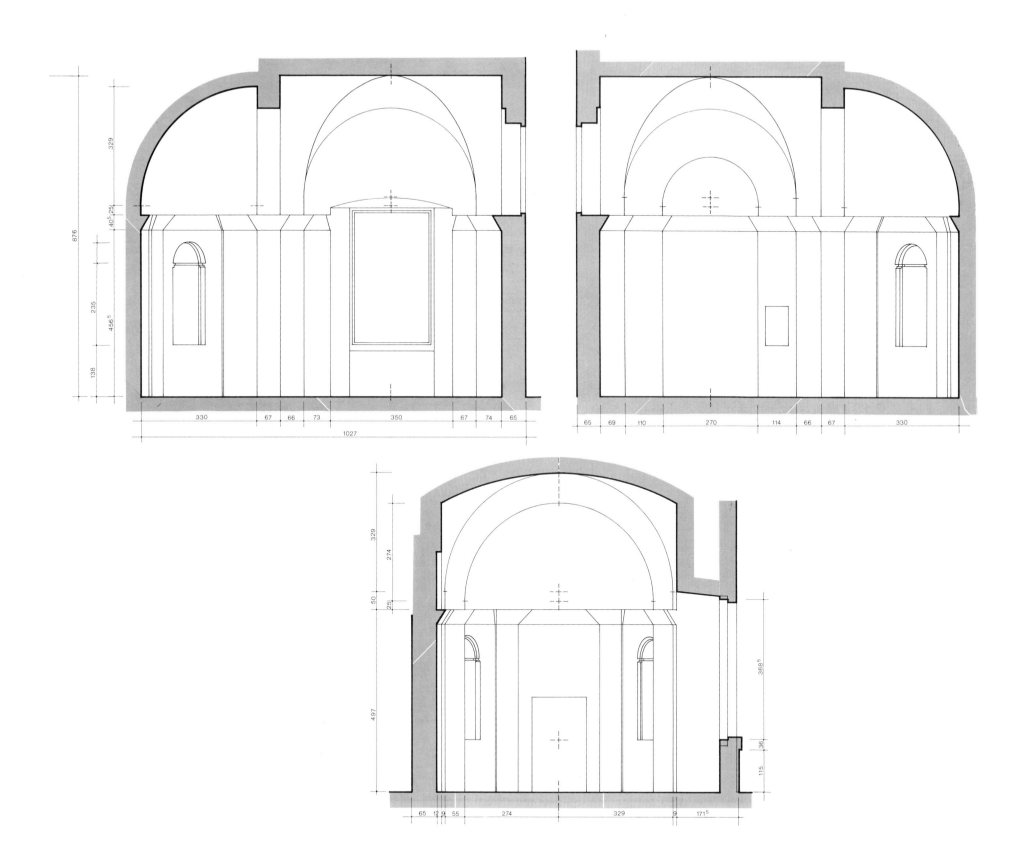

Fig. 53 GD: reconstructed plan of complex

See paragraphs 16 to 18, plus figs 27 and 28 *supra*.

Based upon the U 273 A plan and Raphael's description, the reconstruction departs from the former in several respects. In the first place, the court-side windows of the large hall and of the main room in the North-West apartment have been placed on axis with the corresponding façade windows whereas, in the original plan, the first are slightly offset, not only in relation with the second but also with the ordonnance of the court, the consequence being that they are treated as shams. The anomaly comes from a discrepancy in wall thicknesses. In the U 273 A plan, the length of the hall is marked 82 ½ palmi, the width of the main room in the North-West apartment is marked 40 and the length of the smaller rooms is marked 38, the thickness of the wall separating the larger from the smaller rooms thus coming out as 82 ½ less 78, being 40 plus 38 palmi, or 4 ½ palmi. But the wall belongs in a series of six transversal walls of which three are marked as being 5 palmi thick and it so happens that, by making them all the same, the windows become opposite on both sides of the rooms while those on the court-side fall in line with the centres of the columnated bays in which they belong. Moreover, putting the length of the hall at 83 palmi, the unification of the wall thicknesses brings the length of the superstructure façade up to 444 palmi whereas, in the design put into execution, it comes to 333. The 83 palmi length has therefore been implemented in the reconstructured plan, thicknesses of 5 ½ and 4 palmi being retained for the main longitudinal walls and the partition walls respectively.

The other major differences are the following: the external diameter of the towers has been brought up from 40 to 60 palmi, the latter being the dimension specified by Raphael, a set of ramps has been inserted into the central court to comply with the conjecture put forth in paragraphs 17 and 18 *supra*, and the circumjacencies of the North tower have been redesigned to conform with the enlargement of the latter, (the arrangement adopted bying aimed at providing the tower-enclosed chapel with a forecourt: an alternative would be to run the terrace garden wall straight down to the tower, and rotate the interior of the chapel to make the doorway accessible from the platform at the foot of the wall.) On the contrary, the following particulars are the same as in the U 273 A plan. The entrance court and the central court are both 110 by 220 palmi while the terrace-garden is 110 by 265, the difference of 45 palmi coming from the unequal widths of the South-East and North-West sides of the court, the first of which is 95 palmi, the second, 50. The width of the North east part of the superstructure is 71 palmi, except at the centre of the loggia where it reaches 72 palmi owing to the extrusion of the tribune-like arcaded bay.

A reconstruction of the North-West façade of the entrance court is shown in Fig. 54 *infra*. The same ordonnance prevails in the central court, and it remains the main constituent in the North-East façade. Rhythmed by 6 palmi thick columns, either semi-engaged or standing free before related pilasters, it comprizes bays of three different widths: 24 palmi for those enclosing a portal, 14 palmi for those enclosing

either a doorway or a window and, in the court only, 9 palmi for those enclosing either a niche or, in the case of the nymphaeum, a small doorway. In the North-East façade, reconstructed in Fig. 55B, the 14 palmi bays are incorporated into those of the big radiating arcades whereas, in the North-West façade, they are completely absent.

The remarkable distribution of the service quarters, inscribed D, E, F, G, is commented upon in paragraph 16 *supra*. The length of the entrance portico is the same as that of the ensuing lobby : separated by a 5 palmi thick arcade, they are both 41 palmi long, the total coming to 87 palmi. Going by the thickness of the portico columns in the U 273 A plan, it looks as though they were meant to be 4 palmi thick, thereby implying a height equal to that of the whole interval between the pavement and the underside of the barrel vault surmounting them, or 31 palmi, which corresponds to 7 1/2 times the diameter of the column, plus 1 palmo. Amounting to 9 2/3 palmi, the intercolumniation would have corresponded to twice the diameter of the column plus 5/12ths, thereby complying with the classical rule of 2 1/4 to 2 1/2 diameter spacings. The stairwell lying between room G and the lobby is 18 by 40 palmi. To reach the attic storey, 49 1/2 palmi up, 66 risers of 3/4 palmo would have been required which, associated with 2 palmi treads, would have called for the insertion of 5 flights of 12 steps, plus a returned step at the upper floor level.

The diameter of the domical vault, in the large hall, has been set at 45 palmi in order to make the split pillars which support it sufficiently solid, the depth of the arcades thus coming to 19 palmi longitudinally and 9 transversally. The rooms marked H, I, and J are 40 palmi square while those marked K and L, as well as the garden portico, are 28 by 51. The stairway rising between the last set of rooms and the portico is shown with paired flights of 17 steps, with 2 palmi treads, providing 18 risers of 3/4 palmo each. Since the internal ground level would have been 41 1/4 palmi down, a returned step plus 3 flights would have been required to reach the superstructure level whereas an additional 3 flights plus 10 steps would have allowed one to reach the attic storey.

The walled-in garden is 54 by 108 palmi, against 55 by 110 in the U 273 A plan, the width amounting in both cases to half the length. There are two reasons for the discrepancy. One comes from the generalization of a 5 palmi thickness in the six transversal walls. The other from the necessity of making the courtside garden wall and the external wall of the corridor no thinner than 4 palmi, the garden-side wall of the corridor no thinner than 2 palmi and the actual corridor no narrower than 7 palmi, the total coming to 17 palmi which, deducted from 71, leaves 54 for the width of the garden, the comparative constriction of the corridor being compensated by the provision of an additional access to the tower via the garden. Regarding the towers, yet another discrepancy lies in the greater size of their internal diameter, the present one being 48 palmi against 30 in the original plan.

The North-East loggia is as long as the oppositioned stairwells plus the width of the cross-vaulted passage lying between them, that is 140 palmi. The spine-walled stairways are 24 palmi wide and comprise each a returned flight of steps : see paragraph 18 and Note 22 *supra*, the steps being 11 palmi wide and the spine-wall 2. The loggia is 32 palmi wide, the depth of the cross-vaulted passage is 26 and, from the court-side wall

down, the arcades are 4, 4 plus 1 and 5 palmi thick, the width of the whole structure reaching the 72 palmi mentioned earlier on. The apposition of the two apse-concluded naves formed by the double stairwell and the loggia, the widths of which relate in terms of 3 to 4, is quite spectacular in plan form. To remain so spatially, the effect would have been dependent upon the double stairwell being uniformly vaulted and, consequently, the two stairways being stopped at superstructure level. In the U 273 A plan, the filling of the windows in the North-West part of the stairwell makes one shudder at the thought that someone may have had the idea of continuing the stairway upward.

Rooms A and B, described by Raphael as meant to have a width equal to three quarters of their length, are 28 $\frac{1}{2}$ by 38 palmi and the only ones to have been given the same dimensions in the execution design. Room C is 40 by 60 palmi. The plan of the North-West portico is essentially the same as that of the loggia except that, at its North-East end, it is concluded by a plane wall, at the opposite end by a rather petty-looking nymphaeum backed by a service corridor and a downward-going stairway. The plan includes a private latrine attached to room A.

The fishpond is not the least remarkable part of the design. The stairways are 11 palmi wide, each one being made to incorporate 6 flights of steps which, with 2 palmi treads and $\frac{2}{3}$ palmo risers, give the fishpond platform a length of 92 palmi and place it 36 palmi below the terrace-garden, or 6 palmi off the ground. The actual pond is 42 by 192 palmi: backed by a wall bearing a 9 bay Doric ordonnance and surmounted by a pair of 5 bay garden screens, it is bordered on its three other sides by a quadruple row of bench-like degrees each of which, 3 palmi deep, might have been 1 $\frac{1}{2}$ palmi high. As observed in paragraph 32, not 26, the lay-out is in marked contrast with that which was adopted.

The theatre, substantially smaller than that shown in the U 314 A plan, is essentially a piece of garden architecture in the shape of an odeum, not of a theatre. A semi-circular stage would probably have been founded upon the peripheral wall of the nymphaeum bordering the central court, and surmounted by a semi-circular colonnade similar to the underlying one. It must be admitted that the arrangement bears a far closer relationship to the general design than that which superseded it.

The plan which has just been surveyed is a superb example of classical composition. Moreover, notwithstanding the problem discussed in paragraphs 17 and 18 *supra*, and considering the absence of ancillary accommodation in the North-West part of the superstructure as signifying that the three-room apartment was destined for day-time occupation only, the plan is admirably suited to its purpose. To the observations made in this respect might be added the following : since the master-kitchen and its dependencies lie under the North-West apartment, the North-West portico would have been serviced via the stairway emerging at the back of the nymphaeum whereas the guest apartments, the main hall, the North-East loggia and the North-West apartment would have been via the cryptoportico and the main stairway. But the essential conclusion to be drawn at the close of this review is that it was probably to give the North-West part of the superstructure a full-time occupational function that the circular court was introduced into the design.

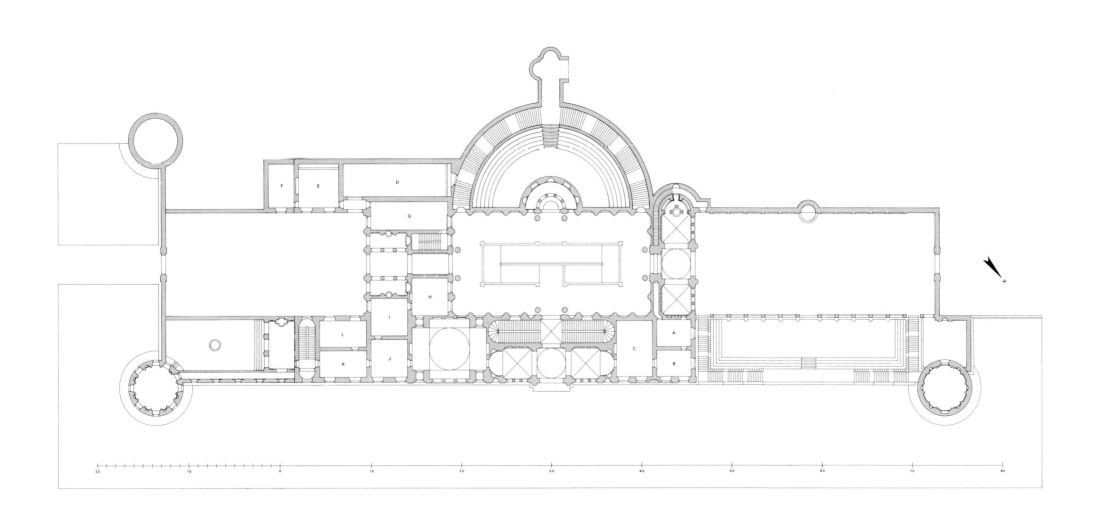

Fig 54 GD : Reconstructed ordonnance of the superstructure

See Figs 28, 47 and 53 supra.

The reconstructed ordonnance is naturally based upon that of the execution design. The column of the first is slightly shorter than the pilaster of the second. It is 53 palmi high, instead or 53 $2/3$, whereas the height of the pedestal is slightly superior, with 4 $1/2$ palmi instead of 4 $1/3$. The entablature is the same but the thickness of the main impost cum string-course is 3 palmi instead of 2 $5/6$. The reason for the changes is twofold. In the first place, it seems evident that the heights of column and pilaster were accorded to form a total of 58 palmi. In the second, in the case of a first approach such as this, there is every likelihood that it was a simple system of proportions which prevailed. Altogether the height of the order comes to 71 palmi instead of 7 $11/2$.

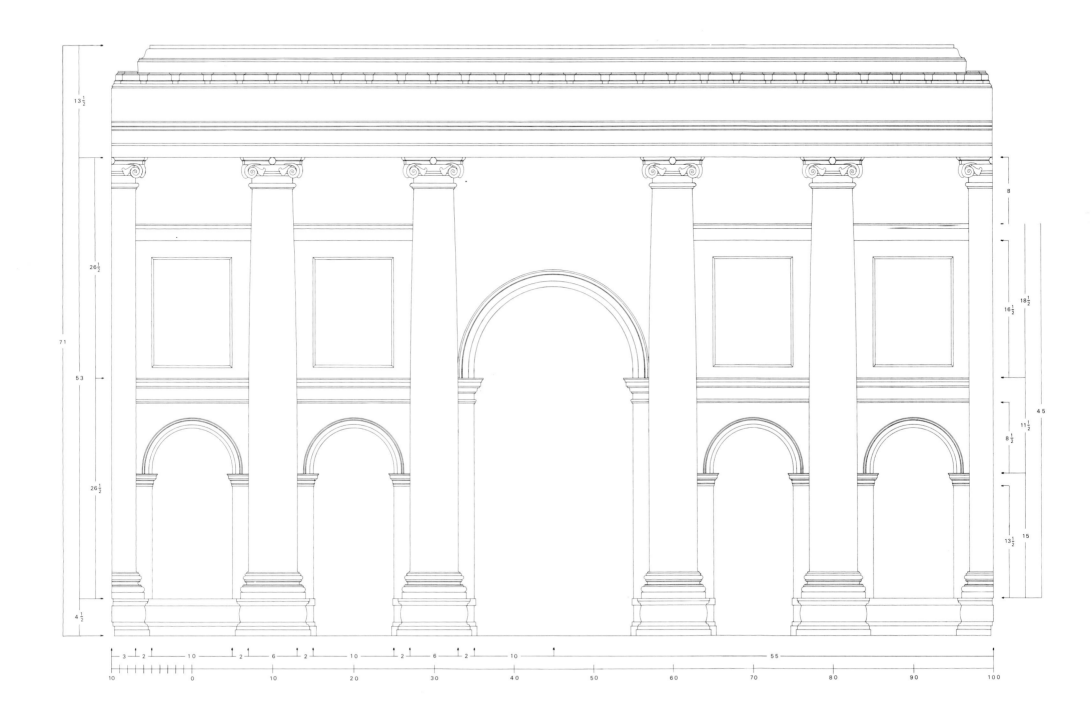

Fig. 55 GD : Reconstructed elevations of the complex

A – South east front

B – Central part of North east front

This reconstruction and those which follow, in Figs 55 B, 56 A and B, are to be considered in relation with paragraphs 14 to 18 and the commentary to Fig. 53 *supra*. The entrance portal and the large towers are in keeping with Raphael's description whereas the crenallation corresponds to his idea of providing a semblance of defence.

Excepting the arcaded windows and the predominance of the string-course underlying the entablature, the elevation is very similar to that of the execution project. Taken from the outer edge of one terminal pilaster to that of the other, the length is 320 palmi against 333. Including the court-side wing shown in Fig. 56 *infra*, it is 444 palmi.

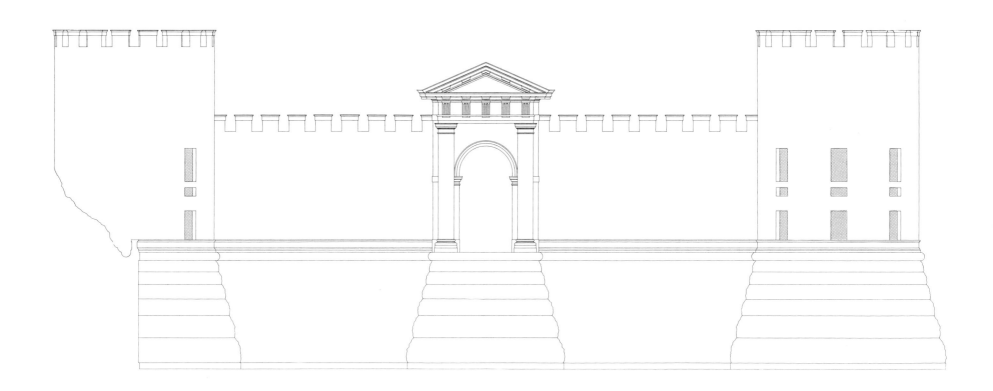

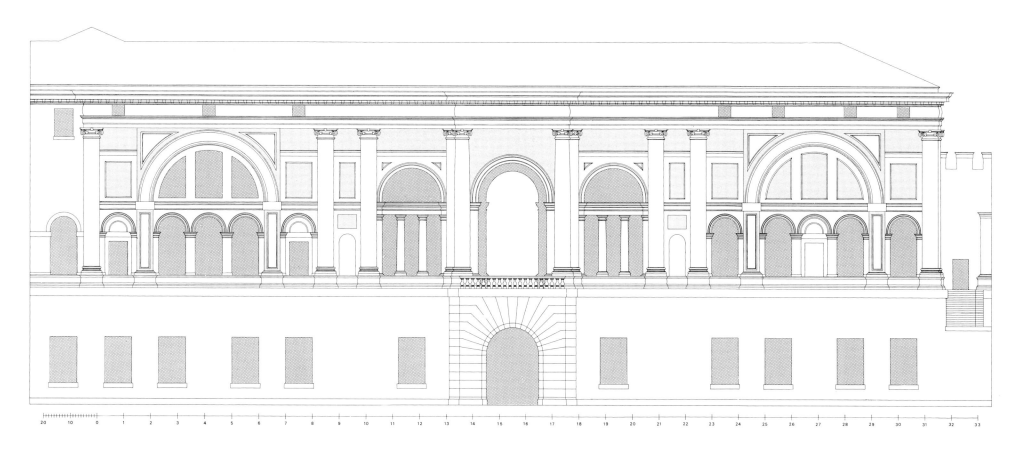

Fig. 56 GD : Reconstructed elevations of the complex

A – South east part of North-East front
B – North west part of North-East front

The ordonnance at the back of the fishpond and the screen surmounting it conform with the U 273 A plan. The diameter of the engaged columns is 4 palmi while their inter-axial spacing is 19 palmi in the side bays, 24 palmi at the centre. The principle of the screen wall is the same as in the garden of the Duchess, in the Palace of Urbino.

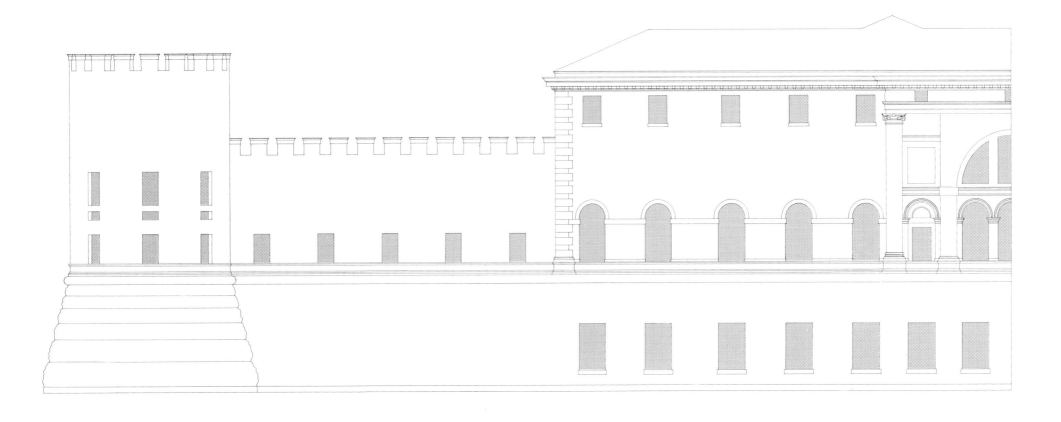

Section 6: The project tentatively brought to completion

57 – GD: General plan
58 – GD: NW half of superstructure, external elevations
59 – GD: Elevations of the complex
        A – South-East front
        B – Central part of North-East front
60 – GD: Elevations of the complex
        A – South-East part of North-East front
        B – North-West part of North-East front
61 – GD: North-West end of entrance court
62 – GD: South-East end of entrance court
63 – GD: Entrance court, junction of lower and upper elevations
64 – GD: North-West end of walled-in garden
65 – GD: Cross-section of entrance portico and lobby
66 – Bird's eye view of theatre and circular court in 1984 model

Fig. 57 GD : General plan

For all Figs concerning the tentative completion scheme, see paragraphs 30 to 34 *supra*.

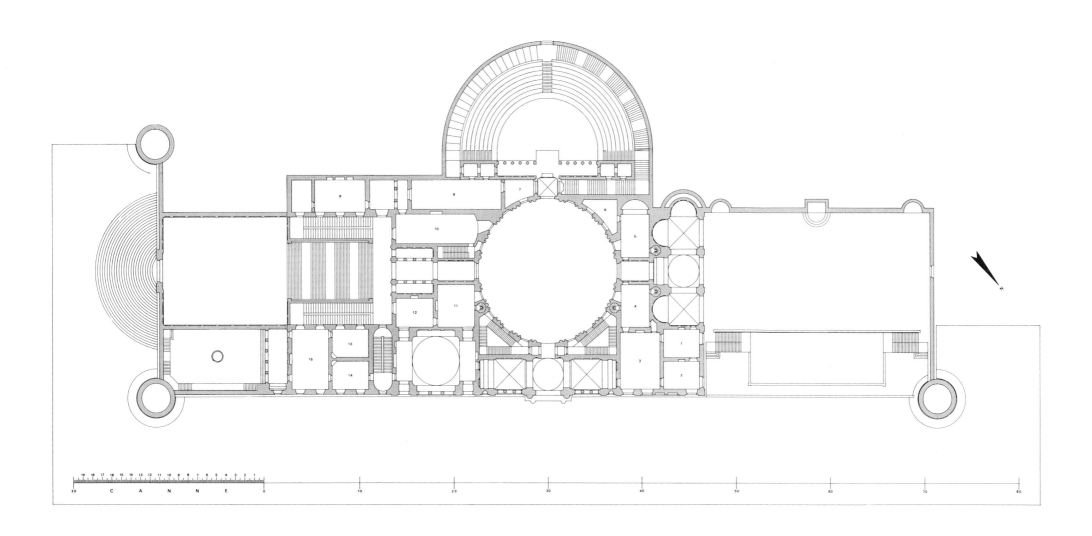

Fig. 58 GD : North-West half of superstructure, external elevations

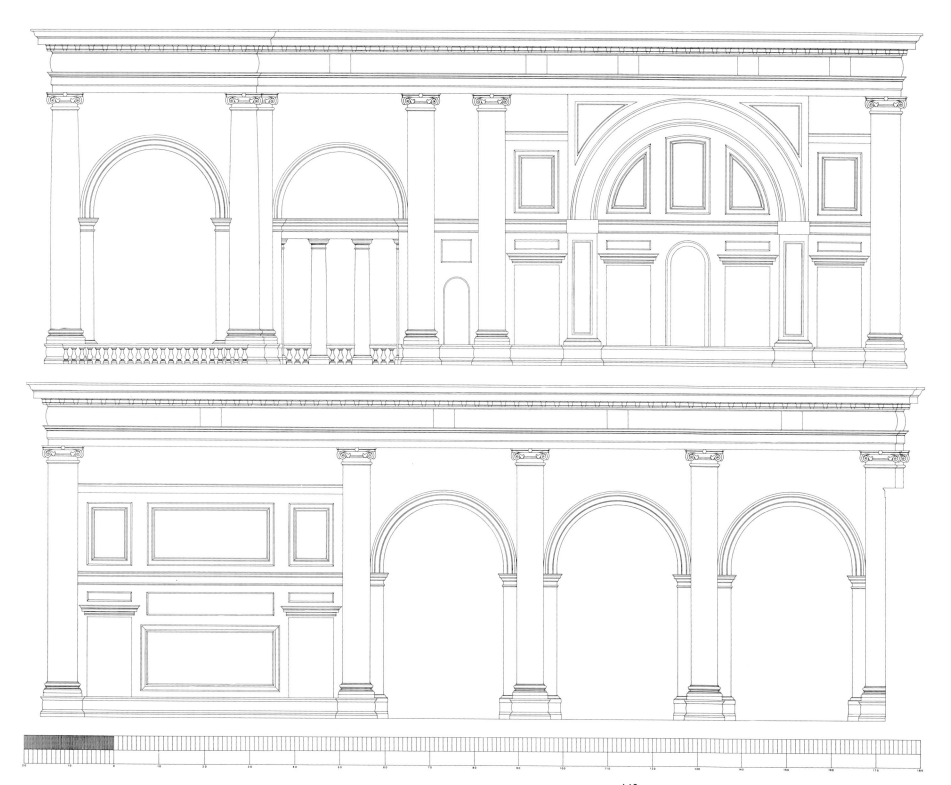

163

Fig. 59 GD : Elevations of complex
A – South-East front
B – Central part of North-East front

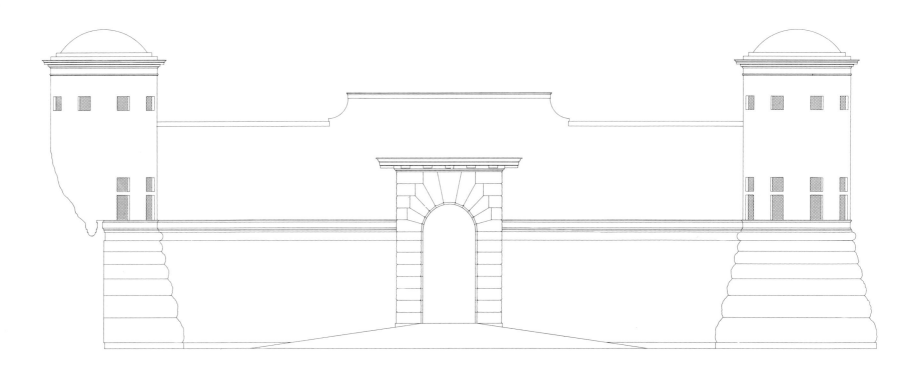

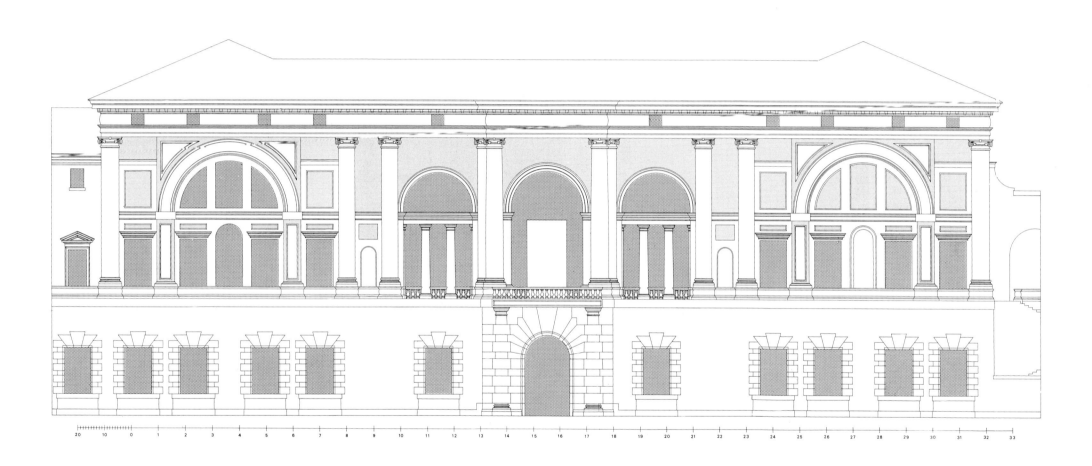

Fig. 60 GD : Elevations of complex
A – South-East part of North-East front
B – North-West part of North-East front

The outlined extension of the court-side wing answers the observation made in paragraph 34 *supra*.

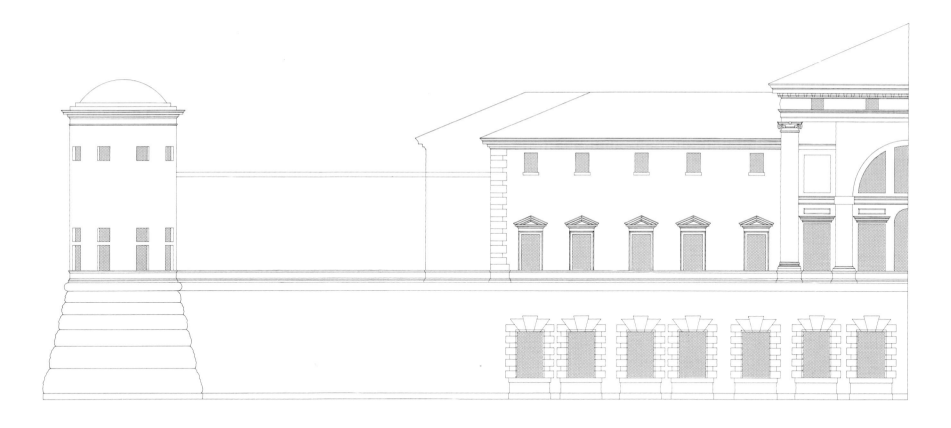

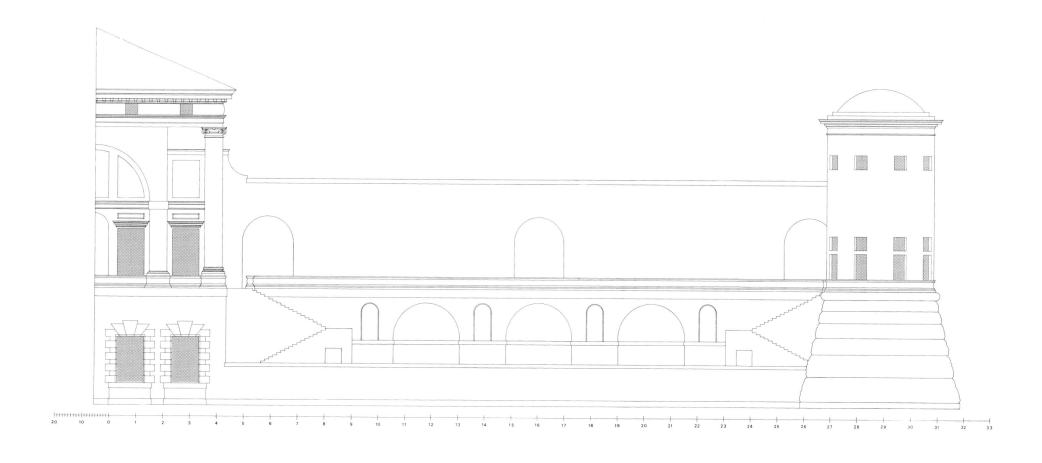

Fig. 61 GD : North-West end of entrance court

The enormous-looking window apertures, on either side of the entrance portal, are the same as in the North-East and North-West façades of the superstructure.

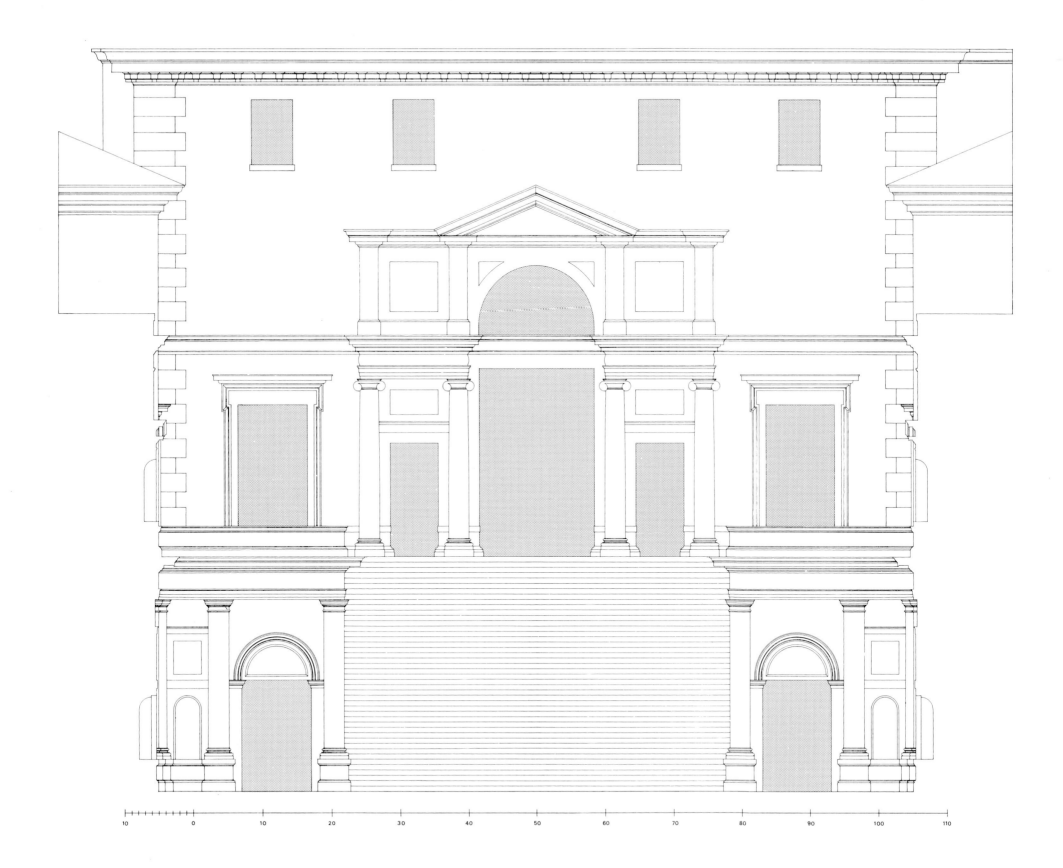

Fig. 62 GD : *South-East end of entrance court*

The elevation corresponds to the U 314 A plan whereas the motif of the niche-surmounted Doric pilasters is taken from the Palazzo Branconio da L'Aquila façade : see Figs 33 and 35 *supra*.

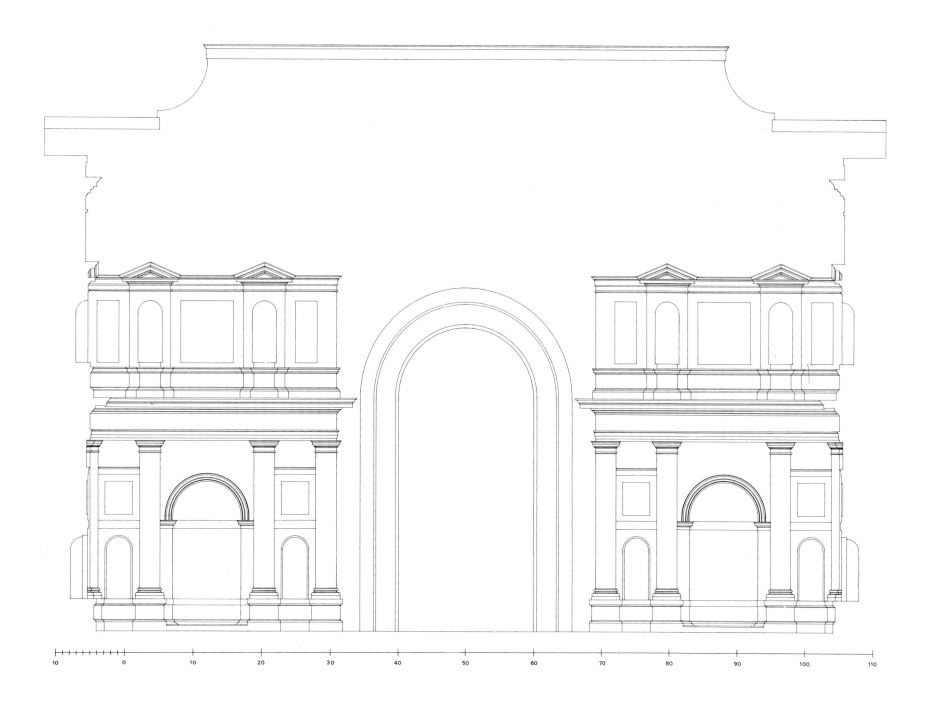

10   0   10   20   30   40   50   60   70   80   90   100   110

171

Fig. 63 GD : Entrance court, junction of lower and upper elevations

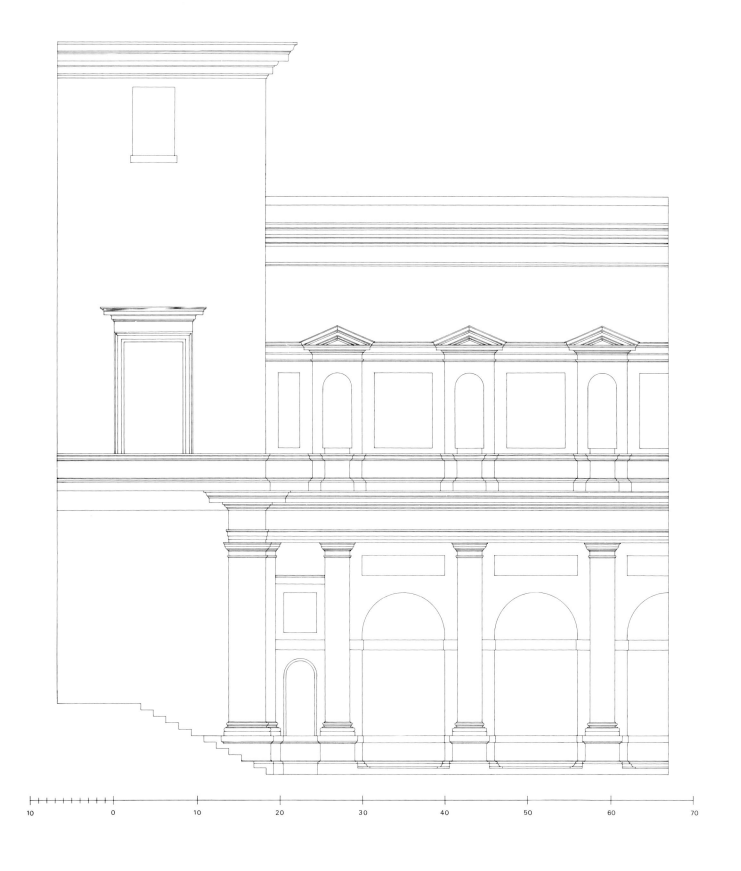

10   0   10   20   30   40   50   60   70

Fig. 64 GD : North-West end of walled-in garden

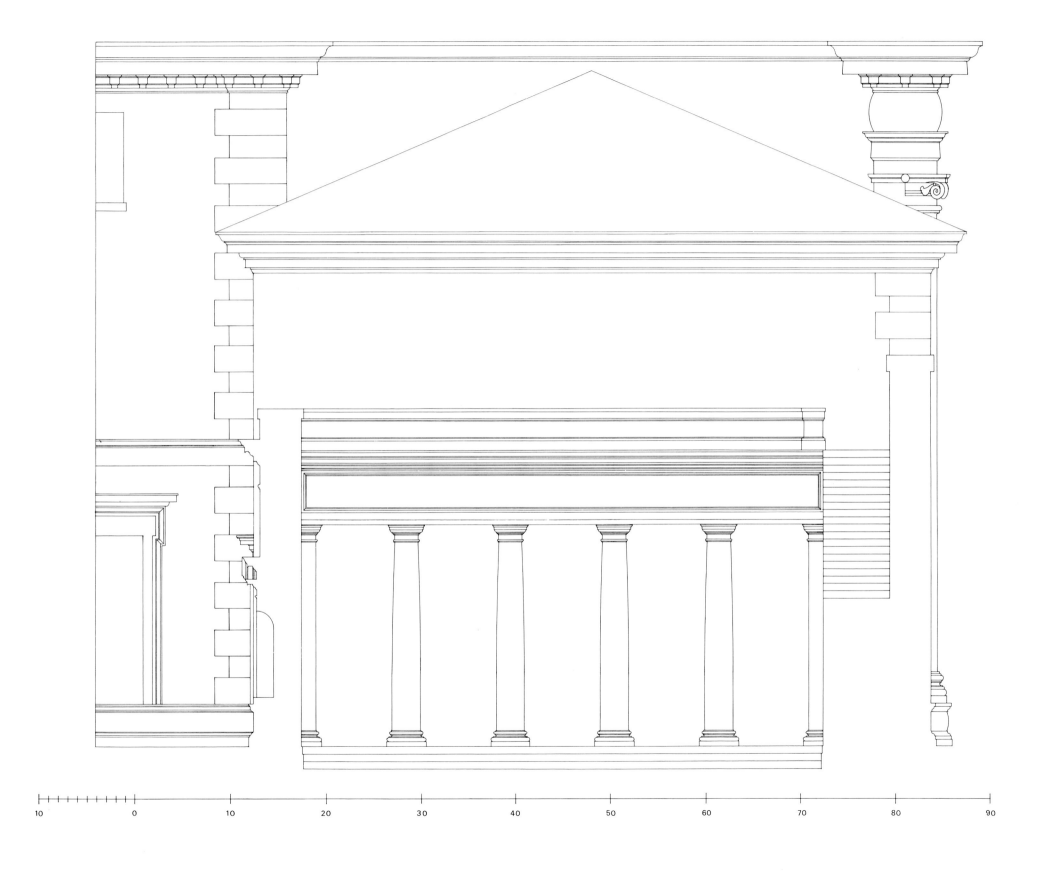

Fig. 65 GD : Cross-section of entrance portico and lobby

Fig. 66 Bird's eye view of theatre and circular court in 1984 model

The model is that referred to in the Prologue. The opening in the back-wall of the theatre is mentioned in Raphael's description. It has the advantage of instoring a visual continuity between the theatre and the circular court. Not particularly commendable from an acoustical point of view, the opening was to have been obstructed, during performances, with painted stage settings.

Glossary

Abacus	The top part of a capital, in the shape of a square slab or tablet, upon which rests the entablature.
Aedicular	The attribute of a doorway, a niche or a window, enclosed between two engaged columns and surmounted by an entablature, pedimented or not.
Apsidal recess	A large semi-circular wall concavity, hemispherically vaulted.
Arcade	An arched opening, or a series of arched openings.
Architrave	The lower member of an entablature.
Archivolt	A semi-circular band, moulded or not, which serves to enhance the curvature of an arch.
Astragal	A small moulding of semi-circular section.
Baluster	One of a series of short moulded pillars forming a see-through parapet known as a balustrade. There are two main types of balusters : the single-bulbed and the double-bulbed, the first being stockier than the second.
Bed-mould	The lower part of a cornice, incorporating a series of mouldings supporting the corona.
Canna	Unit of measurement, see Appendix II.
Cavetto	A concave sweep at the top and bottom of a column shaft or of any flat surface such as that of a die.
Composite	The last and most elaborate of the classical orders, in which the capital incorporates an abacus supported by four pairs of contiguously angled Ionic volutes, unattached and springing from an echinus which surmounts a circular grouping of acanthus, olive or laurel leaves. Applying to an order combining Ionic and Corinthian elements, the term is also used to designate any composition making a free use of the classical repertory.
Corinthian	The order in which the capital incorporates an abacus supported by four pairs of contiguously angled volutes emerging vertically from a circular grouping of acanthus, olive or laurel leaves, each volute presenting on either of its internal sides a shorter outshoot forming with its opposite an assemblage marking the major orthogonal axes of the capital.
Cornice	The upper member of an entablature.
Corona	The slab-like protruding part of a cornice, overlying the bed-mould and surmounted by a cymatium.

Cyma	A double curve moulding in which the upper curve is concave, the lower curve convex.
Cymatium	The top part of a cornice, overlying the corona, usually terminated by a cyma-supported fillet.
Dado	The lower part of a wall, made to look like a pedestal.
Diaeta	A secluded place of retirement or social intercourse.
Dentil	One of a series of small rectangular blocks figuring in the bed-mould of the Ionic, Corinthian and Composite cornices.
Die	The flat part of a dado or of a pedestal : it may be pulvinated.
Doric	The first and simplest of the classical orders, in which the capital incorporates an abacus supported by an echinus usually resting upon a fillet or series of fillets overlying the shaft of the column by means of a cavetto.
Echinus	The cushion-like element supporting the abacus in the Doric capital, the interconnection of the paired volutes in the Ionic capital and the independent volutes in the Composite capital.
Entablature	The horizontal conclusion to a colonnade or a wall. An entablature is usually composed of three members, the cornice, the frieze and the architrave, but it often happens that the frieze is omitted.
Exaedra	A large concave structure, or part of a structure, usually semi-circular, either open to the sky or hemispherically vaulted.
Fascia	One of the two or three flat bands that usually subdivide an architrave.
Fillet	A thin flat band used to top a moulding or to separate two mouldings.
Frieze	The median member of an entablature : usually flat, it may be pulvinated.
Impost	A wall extrusion, usually moulded, the function of which is to support the archivolt of an arcade.
Intercolumniation	The interval between the lower part of two consecutive column shafts.
Intonaco	The final coating spread upon a wall.
Ionic	The order in which the capital incorporates an abacus resting upon the interconnection of paired volutes straddling an echinus.
Lintel	Horizontal beam-like element spanning the void of a doorway or window.
Loggia	A covered arcade or colonnade, raised off the ground.
Minuto	The smallest subdivision in the palmo: see Appendix 2.
Modillion	One of a series of brackets or consoles figuring in the bed-mould of the Corinthian and Composite cornices where they overlie the dentils.
Module	Either the diameter or the radius of a column measured at the bottom of the shaft. Generally subdivided into 24 or 36 parts in the first case, 12 or 18 in the

	second, the module is the unit used in the working out of all the dimensions in the order.
Mullion	A vertical element whereby the void of a window is divided into two equal parts.
Niche	A small semi-circular wall concavity, hemispherically concluded.
Nymphaeum	A monumental fountain or series of fountains.
Ogee	A double curve moulding in which the upper curve is convex, the lower curve concave.
Oncia	The main subdivision in the palmo:: see Appendix 2.
Order	A system of forms and proportions applying to a columnar structure. There are five classical orders : Tuscan, Doric, Ionic, Corinthian and Composite, each being susceptible of certain variations, particularly the last
Ordonnance	An arrangement of architectural parts, a composition.
Palmo	Unit of measurement, see Appendix 2.
Parapet	A waist-high wall preventing people from falling down from a height.
Pedestal	The independent support of a free-standing column or the wall extrusion supporting an engaged column : it consists of a die set between a base and a cornice.
Plinth	The lower element in the base of a column. Also, the moulded base of a dado.
Portico	A covered arcade or colonnade lying at ground level.
Pulvinated	The condition of a flat surface, such as that of a die or a frieze, having been made to bulge out.
Quoin	One of a series of extruded stones, usually rusticated, which serve to enhance the corners of a building or enter into the composition of doorway and window surrounds.
Scotia	A small concave moulding, fillet bordered, set between two tori : see Torus.
Skirting-block	An extruded block serving to interrupt the moulding of a surround at the foot of a doorway or window.
Spandrel	The flat wall area surrounding an arch. The term also applies to the bent, vault-bearing element found between two contiguous arches.
String-course	A horizontal band, moulded or not, running across a wall.
Stucco	A fine plaster composed of gypsum and pulverized marble, used for fashioning mouldings and decorative motifs as well as for coating walls.
Surbase	The railing of a dado.
Torus	A moulding of semi-circular section used mostly in column bases.
Transom	A horizontal element subdividing the void of a window into two unequal parts, the lower being generally the larger.

Travertine	A white concretionary limestone, usually semi crystalline and quite hard. It is the choice medium for carved ornamentation.
Tufa	A light porous stone, formed of pulverulent matter consolidated, either calcareous or volcanic : a cheap material, it was used extensively throughout Italy, often associated with reinforcing brickwork.
Tuscan	A simplified form of the Doric order.
Volute	A spiral scroll.
Xystus	Defined as follows in Appendix 1, paragraph 16, Note 1 : Xystus is an ancient Greek word designating the covered racing track in a gymnasium. In Rome, at the time of the younger Pliny, it had come to mean a formally planted garden, usually associated with a portico.